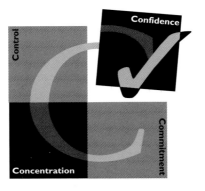

Building Self-confidence

Preface

Many factors contribute to sports performance. In addition to the physical, technical and strategic demands of sport, performers must be able to remain focused, maintain emotional control, sustain self-confidence, and constantly apply themselves in both training and competition. In your own sport, you will undoubtedly be able to recognise the mental demands placed on performers. Meeting these demands may be relatively easy when things are going well but less so during times of difficulty (eg poor form, distractions, injury). Coaches typically identify a range of mental qualities that seem to underpin successful sports performance – qualities encompassed in the four Cs: commitment, confidence, concentration and control.

Confidence certainly plays a crucial role in success in sport. This exciting new booklet, **Building Self-confidence,** will help coaches and performers develop, maintain and if necessary, restore confidence. It includes a wealth of ideas that can be readily integrated into everyday coaching practice without making substantial changes to existing sessions and programmes. Advice is offered on how to use goal-setting, imagery, positive self-talk and routines to help your performers develop and maintain a positive attitude and healthy belief in themselves and their own ability.

The pack is divided into two parts:

Part One contains three chapters, is written in home study format and provides an overview of mental skills training, an introduction to self-confidence training and guidance on the importance of performance profiling in assessing performer needs. These chapters will help you to:

- identify the contribution of the fundamental mental skills to overall sports performance
- assess your knowledge of basic mental skills training methods
- explain the importance of self-confidence to performance in your sport
- profile performers to identify their strengths and weaknesses.

Part Two consists of six practical mental skill programmes – many involve working directly with your performer/s either within or outside your normal coaching sessions. These practical sessions will help you to build self-confidence through using profiling, goal-setting, positive self-talk, imagery and routines. By working through the programmes with your performers, you should be able to identify:

- ways that mental skills can improve self-confidence
- how mental skills training can be incorporated into your overall training programmes
- a strategy (action plan) to strengthen and maintain self-confidence.

A final summary with follow-up references concludes the pack.

This is an essential pack for coaches and performers looking for the winning edge – it may also be of benefit to sport psychologists, team managers and support staff. The following icons are used in the pack.

Key to symbols used in the text:

     An activity.

     Approximate length of time to be spent on the activity.

Contents

PART ONE

Chapter One: Overview of Mental Skills Training

1.0 What's in it for You?

The field of mental skills training is still relatively new to many coaches, although the importance of the mind in sport has been recognised for many years. Sport involves a mind game as well as a physical performance and without developing qualities such as confidence, commitment, concentration and control, peak performance will remain an unattainable dream for most performers.

Before examining self-confidence in more detail, it is helpful to consider the effect of mental factors on sports performance and help you assess your experience and knowledge in the use of mental training skills. This chapter provides an overview and by the end, you should be able to:

- identify the contribution of the fundamental mental qualities (the 4Cs) to overall sports performance in your sport

- assess your knowledge and experience of basic mental skills training methods

- communicate to your performers the value of mental practice to improve their sports performance.

1.1 Importance of Mental Qualities

You are probably already aware of the influence of mental factors on sports performance – in learning new skills as well as in producing consistent high level performance. How often is a competition won by the performer who:

- handles pressure better

- is totally committed to a tough training regime

- maintains concentration in spite of distractions

- remains confident in spite of setbacks?

The first activity will help you to consider the impact of mental factors on your performers.

ACTIVITY 1

1 Reflect on a recent coaching session or competition in which one of your performers:

- performed well beyond expectation
- significantly under performed.

2 List all the reasons why you felt the performer over- or under-achieved:

Over-achieved because:	Under-achieved because:

You may find you have listed some reasons that are directly concerned with the performer's mental state (eg frustrated by weather conditions). Alternatively you may find some of the reasons are essentially physical, technical or tactical (eg skills broke down under the opposition's pressure).

3   To what extent might these reasons result in changes in mental state? (eg Did the fear of repeated injury influence self-confidence? Was the performer's focus too much on the opposition rather than own performance?) To what extent did the outcome influence the performer's:

- assessment of performance?   not at all   somewhat   a great deal

- subsequent mental state or approach
  to training and competition?   not at all   somewhat   a great deal

List any mental factors you believe might have contributed to the over- or under-achievement or subsequent mental state:

-

-

-

4   Identify the key situations in your sport when these factors might be important (eg at the start, at a penalty, following an injury):

-

-

-

Now turn over.

— 3 —

2   Some of the reasons listed to explain over- and under-achievement might appear in the following chart:

Over-achieved because:	Under-achieved because:
Sticking to agreed game plan	Lack of fitness
Good mental and physical preparation	Poor weather conditions or facilities
Maintaining focus and emotional control	Unfavourable officiating decisions
Selecting appropriate equipment (eg club, racing tyres)	Injury or fear of injury
Ideal conditions (eg no wind, dry pitch)	Strength of opponent
Adapting to changing circumstances (eg score line, opponent's tactics)	Breakdown in skills
High confidence due to good fitness level	Poor tactical decisions
	Choked at a critical point
	Distracted (eg by crowd, officials, opponent, incident)
	Failure by other team members

3   The sort of mental factors you may have listed could probably be summarised under the 4Cs:

- Commitment (ie will to win, toughness)
- Control of emotions (eg of anxiety, anger, frustration)
- Concentration (ie focus)
- Confidence (ie positive attitude, self-belief).

4   Consider your answers by reviewing the following specific situations that in some sports might make significant demands on mental qualities:

- At the start of a race, game or event.
- The end of a race, last ten minutes of a game, final event (eg last jump, last piece of apparatus).
- Following a foul, an unfavourable officiating decision, an injury, equipment failure.
- Before a difficult or particularly crucial situation (eg the jump following a no-jump, the most difficult piece of apparatus, at a penalty, in extra time, at a scrum close to your own try line).

You will probably have recognised that mental factors contribute significantly to performance in your sport[1]. To illustrate the potential significance of mental qualities, read the following example from tennis.

Sampras versus Moya, Australian Open 1997

Total play time: 87 minutes
Action time: 17 minutes
Time between action: 70 minutes (potential thinking time)

During these 70 minutes, there was the opportunity for both negative and positive thoughts, feelings and self-talk; plenty of time to think oneself into or out of the match.

---

[1]   If you need further guidance in identifying the contribution of mental factors to your sport, you are recommended to **Mental Skills: An Introduction for Sports Coaches,** available from Coachwise Ltd (0113 231 1310).

1.2 Mental Training Techniques

Most competitors use a variety of mental techniques – often as a result of experience or trial and error rather than through teaching. They have learnt strategies to help them cope with difficult situations both in a sports context and perhaps in life more generally (eg dealing with examinations, interviews, work pressures, relationships). Coaches can accelerate and enhance this process by introducing and systematically developing appropriate techniques for specific occasions. You may already use or be familiar with a number of techniques. Try Activity 2.

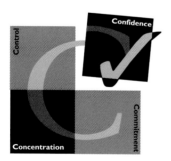

ACTIVITY 2

1   List any mental skills you or your performers use (with or without your input) or may wish to use to improve the mental qualities listed in the left hand column. An example skill for each quality is given to help you:

Qualities	Skills
Commitment	Goal setting
Concentration	Imagery
Control	Relaxation training
Confidence	Positive thinking

2   Describe in more detail the skills you have listed under **confidence:**

Now turn over.

1   *Table 1 provides an overview of the type of skills that can be used to strengthen each quality:*

Qualities	Skills
Commitment	Goal setting Refocusing Positive thinking (eg use of positive statements)
Concentration	Imagery Distraction training Developing routines and using crib cards Segmenting performance into easy-to-manage components Simulated competition training
Control	Relaxation training Breathing exercises (eg centring) Cognitive restructuring Positive self-statements Developing routines Simulated competition training
Confidence	Positive thinking Imagery Goal-setting Routines Cognitive restructuring (positive thinking) Simulated competition training

Table 1: Overview of mental qualities and skills

2   *The skills listed under self-confidence will be the focus of subsequent sessions in this pack. You should note that many of the skills in this category also appear elsewhere. This demonstrates the versatility of these skills and the way in which they can be integrated into an overall mental skills strategy.*

If you had any difficulty with this activity or if any of the techniques are new to you, you may find it useful to develop your understanding further before continuing with this pack. You are recommended to the NCF home study pack: **Mental Skills: An Introduction for Sports Coaches** as well as other mental skills packs, available from Coachwise Ltd (0113 231 1310).

1.3 Learning Mental Skills

Whatever skills (mental, technical, physical) you wish your performers to develop, the cyclical process through which they learn, practise and apply the skills remains much the same:

STEP 1 Identify all the factors (or qualities) that can positively affect performance. You may wish to profile your performer's qualities separately in each of the following areas or take a whole performer approach (ie profile your performer's strengths and weaknesses on those qualities deemed most important: technical, tactical, physical, mental qualities).

STEP 2 Identify with each performer, his or her strengths and weaknesses in relation to each quality. This profiling can be recorded using the performance profiling techniques introduced in Section 3.1 (Page 44).

STEP 3 From this profiling, you will be able to determine with each performer the key qualities that will result in the most profound improvements in performance. For example, the key factor might be greater self-confidence, improved power, better decision-making.

STEP 4 Select the most appropriate way to make this improvement – this means you need to know the range of techniques possible and how to use them effectively.

STEP 5 Determine when the technique should be introduced into training, practice and eventually competition (Section 1.4 Page 10). For some mental techniques (eg imagery), there is also the question of when the technique can be used (eg before, during and after the session or competition).

STEP 6 Practise the technique – probably first in training and mock competitions. After a suitable period of time, monitor and assess the effectiveness of the technique. This can involve re-profiling your performer to check for relative improvements. If necessary, the performer may persist with this technique or use an alternative from the range available.

NB Mental skills, like physical skills, take time to learn, practise and use successfully – be patient and build them slowly.

While many performers might recognise the impact of improved technical skills and fitness on sport success, some may be more reluctant to acknowledge the need to commit time and effort to the development of mental qualities. You may need therefore to discuss the potential value of mental skills training with your performers, so they appreciate what you are trying to achieve and how it will improve performance. This enhanced sense of ownership will increase their commitment and adherence to mental training. How and when you do this will depend very much on the performer – his or her profile, expectations and goals, and training programme.

At what point in the training and competition calender should you start to introduce new mental skills? This will depend on a number of factors:

- Your performers' needs and goals, their relative importance of mental skills work to other aspects of training and their current use of mental skills.

- The stage in the training cycle – new mental skills should normally be introduced in the off-season, pre or early phase of the annual programme – not when they are undergoing new or particularly heavy training loads or in the major competition phase.

- Your availability of time – it is best to introduce new mental skills when you have time to talk these through thoroughly with your performers.

ACTIVITY 3

1 Determine when you intend to introduce new mental skills into the training programme for your performer (NB it may be helpful to select one or two performers now with whom you might work as you read through this pack):

Mark these points on the chart provided.

Jan	Feb	Mar	Apr	May	Jun	Jul	Aug	Sep	Oct	Nov	Dec

2 Explain your decision:

1.4 Significance of Self-confidence

The significance of confidence to successful sporting performance will probably have become clear by now. Changes in confidence can make the difference between a top performance and a mediocre one, even when other factors (eg fitness, skill, weather conditions) remain constant. However, confidence can seem a rather elusive and obscure quality, prone to rapid fluctuations even within a competition. What exactly is self-confidence? Why does it fluctuate so readily? How can you quickly recognise shifts and more importantly, what can you do about them? These are the sorts of questions asked by both coaches and performers seeking peak and consistent performance.

ACTIVITY 4

1 Explain what **self-confidence** means to you:

2 Reflect on an occasion when you or your performer experienced high self-confidence and describe under the appropriate heading what you noticed (eg feelings, thoughts, attention focus):

- Occasion (eg a particular competition):

- I noticed (eg more talkative):

3 Reflect on an occasion when you or your performer experienced low self-confidence and describe under the appropriate heading what you noticed (eg feelings, thoughts, attention focus):

- Occasion (eg a particular competition):

- I noticed (eg more talkative):

4 Describe in as much detail as possible the effects of differing levels of self-confidence on performance:

High Self-confidence	Low Self-confidence

Now turn over.

1   *In sport, self-confidence is usually used to refer to a positive attitude and healthy belief in yourself and your ability. More specifically it means:*

- *believing you can meet the challenges you face*

- *believing you can achieve what you have set yourself (eg a short term goal such as winning the next point, a longer term goal such as making selection) – this is based on knowing you have the relevant foundation of skills and talents to achieve your goals*

- *being able to learn from and build on mistakes or failures*

- *feeling in control of the outcome of an event, in control of what happens in your life.*

2/3   *Table 2 describes experiences associated with high and low self-confidence.*

	High Self-confidence	Low Self-confidence
Thoughts	Positive thoughts Thoughts of success	Negative thoughts Thoughts of defeat or failure Doubts
Feelings	Excited Sense of anticipation Elation Calm Ready for action Enjoyment	Tense Sense of dread Not wanting to take part
Focus	Self Task at hand	Others Less relevant factors

Table 2: Behaviour associated with high and low confidence

It is important to remember that self-confidence is personal to the individual. Those performers who appear most calm and assured may be lacking in confidence. How can you tell? You can use these descriptors as prompts to ask your performers about their confidence (eg Do you have thoughts of success or failure at the moment? Do you feel tense or calm?).

4   *However you experience high or low self-confidence, you probably find that:*

- *low self-confidence results in either a lower performance level or a less favourable experience of the performance*
- *high self-confidence results in either a better performance level or a more positive experience of the event.*

Examples of the effects of high and low self-confidence on performance are listed in the following chart:

High Self-confidence	Low Self-confidence
Giving maximum effort	*Lack of effort*
A willingness to take chances	*More likely to give up*
A willingness to react positively to set-backs and learn from the situation	*Playing safe*
High commitment to training	*Misdirected focus*
Strong focus on the task at hand	*Tendency to attribute outcome of events to factors that cannot be controlled (eg luck, environmental conditions).*
Positive attitude and belief in own skills and talent.	

These are the sorts of things you may notice during training sessions or competitions. However, you should remember that you may misinterpret what you see, so it is important to talk specifically to your performers about how they are feeling.

The preceding table is simplistic but provides an overview of some of the common experiences associated with self-confidence. You will note that there can be opposite experiences in any given situation (eg feeling excited or calm when self-confident). All are generalisations – each performer's reaction is unique (and can be very different from others). You will also know from personal experience that self-confidence can be affected by many factors. Try the next activity.

ACTIVITY 5

1   List the major factors that have influenced your self-confidence in sport –
    either as a performer or as a coach. Note whether it increased (↑) or decreased
    (↓) your self-confidence:

Influencing Factor	Self-confidence (↑) / (↓)

2   Try to categorise the influences in your list above. Mark your list according to
    your categorisation.

1   *You probably listed a variety of factors that influence your self-confidence.*
    These can range from very specific factors (eg good previous competitive record
    against a forthcoming opponent, little previous success at a particular venue) to
    more general factors (eg poor build-up and preparation to a season, recent
    improvement in form). Often, the same factor can have a positive or negative
    influence on self-confidence (eg competition results, depending on whether or
    not the outcome is perceived as successful).

2   *You may have noted that your self-confidence can be influenced by personal or*
    internal factors (eg your own form or moods) or external factors (eg team-
    mates, opponents, the crowd, the score line, the conditions). Go back over your
    list and categorise according to whether the factor is internal or external (using
    an I or an E). It is possible to develop strategies to help performers cope with
    both external and internal influences (this will be considered again in Part
    Two). It is important to remember that all these factors (and more) can work
    for or against your performer's self-confidence and affect each of them at
    different times and to different degrees.

1.5   Summary and Further Help

In this chapter, you have been encouraged to reflect on the significance of mental
qualities (especially self-confidence) to success in sport and the potential of mental
skills training techniques. In the next chapter, the techniques that can best be used
to build self-confidence will be considered in more detail. In Chapter Three, the
importance of mental skills work to your performers will be reviewed and you
will be encouraged to profile your performer's strengths and weaknesses. You will
then be able to work through the programmes in Part Two in the order that best
suits your needs and those of your performers.

If the area of mental skills training is fairly new to you, you may find the
following packs helpful:

National Coaching Foundation (1996) **Psychology and performance.** 2nd edition.
Leeds. ISBN 0-947850-24-4.

Sellars, C (1996) **Mental skills: an introduction for sports coaches.** Leeds,
National Coaching Foundation. ISBN 0-947850-34-1.

They are available from Coachwise Ltd (0113 231 1310).

Chapter Two: Building Self-confidence

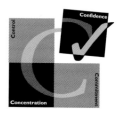

2.0   What's in It for You?

> *Man becomes what he believes himself to be*
> *Mahatma Ghandi*

Success breeds self-confidence. The most successful performers appear to have supreme confidence in their own ability – a confidence based not only on dreams but on a solid foundation of hard work and the knowledge they have the relevant skills and talents to achieve those dreams. Performers who doubt their ability to succeed rarely achieve their potential.

Coaches can play a large part in building a performer's confidence. Good coaches do this in a number of ways – for example, by the way they:

- focus and build on a performer's strengths

- provide positive reinforcement, encouragement and reassurance

- offer critical feedback on performance in a positive and constructive way

- create an environment in which the performer is willing to share doubts and uncertainties

- build a performance plan which progressively builds on each success towards the ultimate goals

- encourage and empower performers to accept responsibility for their own actions and help them develop the skills to gain the mental toughness to cope effectively in any situation.

The way coaches develop programmes and interact with their performers is considered in many other books. This pack focuses primarily on the last point – on helping performers learn a range of mental training techniques to build self confidence. Four skills are presented: goal-setting, self-talk, imagery and routines[1].

---

1   For further help on the mental training techniques, refer to Page 42 or request a Coachwise Catalogue (0113 231 1310) for an up to date listing of new packs.

Each skill will be considered in this chapter to help you:

- explore how it works
- identify the benefits and disadvantages
- assess its relative merits in meeting your needs and those of your performers
- evaluate when and why to use it, and how it can be integrated into regular training programmes and competition.

Like most qualities associated with sports performance, confidence can be improved using various training techniques. That's the good news – however, to be effective, these techniques must be learned, practised, used regularly and integrated into other aspects of performance preparation and competition. It is important to remember as you read, that each mental skill will be best developed by adhering to the leaning principles described in Section 1.3 (Page 9).

This chapter provides a rationale for selecting and implementing the mental skills programmes in Part Two, so it is important to work through it carefully[1].

2.1 Goal-setting

Success increases self-confidence. By adopting a systematic approach to training through goal-setting, you increase your chances of success and the frequency with which success is experienced. By ensuring clear and appropriate feedback is available about successful performance, an upward spiral can be created resulting in increased self-confidence. It is widely recognised, therefore, that one of the most powerful ways of developing confidence is through judicious goal-setting combined with good feedback. The feedback may be directly available through goal achievement or may need to be augmented by the coach to provide specific information about competence. Goals can be set in relation to all aspects of training and competition. They can be structured in training to ensure a high degree of success without making the goals too easy. To maximise competitive success, goals may also need to be focused on the process, not just the outcome (see Types of Goal, Page 25).

Goal difficulty needs to be adjusted to make goals relatively challenging but still sufficiently attainable. Coaches therefore need to create a *success highway* for their performers – recognising that the more success performers experience in sport situations, the greater their self-confidence becomes in those situations.

---

[1] If the information is new to you, you may find it useful to read through the NCF home-study pack **Mental Skills: An Introduction for Sports Coaches,** available from Coachwise Ltd (0113 321 1310).

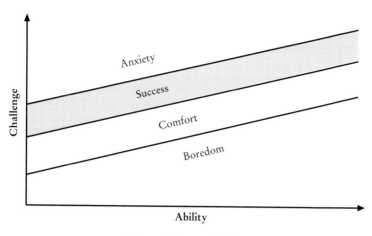

Figure 1: Success highway

Challenge and success

The skill, therefore, is to set goals that provide sufficient challenge to motivate the performer to work to achieve the goal and yet plenty of opportunities for performers to feel competent, experience success and so develop their confidence. Self-confidence is, however, often fragile and in a constant state of change; goals therefore need to be reviewed and adjusted regularly to keep performers in the success lane.

A further difficulty is that all too often performers set themselves goals that are too hard rather than too easy – a goal that is acceptable during training can become unacceptable to the same performer under the stress of competition. Performers who set goals beyond their ability may show short-term improvements in performance. However, in the long-term, consistent failure to achieve the goals will lead to self-criticism and a decrease in self-confidence. In addition, performers are all individuals – they each respond to challenge, success and failure in different ways; and this can dramatically affect their self-confidence. Coaches need to adapt their approach to the unique personality type of the individual and set, review and adjust goals to ensure the performer stays in the success lane – where goal difficulty offers an appropriate level of challenge but sufficient success to build and maintain confidence.

Self-confidence is significantly influenced by success. However, success can mean different things.

ACTIVITY 6

How do you:

- judge success in your sport?

- think your performers judge success in your sport? Ask one or two – you might be surprised.

Now turn over.

You probably found that success can mean different things to different people.

- *Some people judge success as out-performing others (eg beating others, being ranked above others). If the performer starts to lose or believes that future victory is unlikely, confidence will flounder.*

  Coaches and performers who view success in this way, will experience a loss in confidence when win-loss records or placings deteriorate (this is referred to in the literature as normative self-confidence).

- *Others measure success in terms of personal improvement or mastery (eg comparing current performance with own previous performance, personal bests or improvement in an aspect of performance, such as the number of turn-overs recorded, shots on target, speed off the block). Confidence will remain high as long as the performer believes that personal improvements will continue.*

  *Coaches and performers who view success in this way, can maintain confidence even when win-loss records or placings deteriorate (this is referred to in the literature as self-referenced self-confidence). There are a number of advantages for people who judge success in this way – small improvements can provide feelings of success, competency can be judged in personal terms. **They can therefore retain greater control over both the likelihood of success and so their confidence.***

If you are to give your performers some control over self-confidence, it is essential to develop an emphasis on self-referenced self-confidence (ie viewing success in terms of personal improvement rather than through comparison with others). This will allow performers to set goals in training and competition which focus on personal improvement and which, if appropriately set, will provide regular achievement (which in turn provides informational feedback which highlights goal-achievement, success and so self-confidence).

How to set goals

Goal-setting is probably not new to you or your performers. However, goal-setting needs to be done very carefully, if it is to be effective in building confidence and not just mapping out a route – a training programme toward an ultimate goal.

ACTIVITY 7

1   Identify briefly the strengths and weaknesses of the following goals:

Performer's goals
a   I want to reach the final of this tournament.

b   I don't want to get injured this season.

c   I will see if I can score more than ten points.

d   I will be disappointed if I don't make the top three.

Coach's goals
e   I want to get three good sessions in before the next competition.

f   I don't want her to peak too soon.

g   I hope he lasts the match.

2   Explain when and how you set goals to ensure they are effective:

*   When:

*   How:

Now turn over.

1   You will probably notice that some of these goals are rather vague (eg Goal b, Goal f), some are rather negative (eg Goal b, Goals d and g focus on avoiding failure); some are quite specific (eg Goal e is specific but not clearly measurable – what is good?). An effective goal will focus attention on a particular action or actions and encourage the performer to keep trying until the goal is achieved. To aid self-confidence, the goal must also have meaning. Research suggests that by applying certain principles to goal-setting, the goals will be of greater value.

Whatever the goal, it must:

- state the target precisely and be relevant to the performer's needs (specific)
- identify how goal-achievement will be assessed (measurable)
- be agreed by the performer/s trying to achieve it (agreed)
- be perceived as achievable with effort (realistic)
- have a time-frame by which it should be achieved (time-framed)
- challenge and excite the person – it must therefore have meaning and importance (exciting)
- be remembered – best done by committing it to paper, by recording it (recorded)[1].

---

2   To help you set goals that are not only SMARTER, but also appropriate to the needs of your performers, it may help to consider the following process (Figure 2). Whether you work rigorously through this process or not, you probably use goal-setting in many aspects of your coaching. You may have identified goals for the next training session, next competition or the end of the season. Your goals may have focused on technical, tactical, fitness or psychological aspects of your sport.

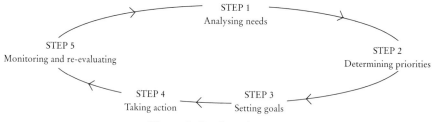

Figure 2: Goal-setting process

---

1   You may already be familiar with the mnemonic SMARTER to help you remember the characteristics of effective goals: Specific, Measurable, Agreed, Realistic, Time-framed, Exciting, Recorded).

STEP 1: Analysing the needs of your sport and performers

With your performers, you can analyse what they must do to be successful at whatever level they participate in their sport. This is where performance profiling techniques can help you identify the qualities needed for success – this may vary between performers – and, with your performers, assess their current level for each one. You can record these qualities and scores on a profile sheet (example on Page 56).

STEP 2: Determining priorities

With your performer, you now have to decide which of the important qualities are high priorities. You may find it useful to rank your goals in order of priority or place target dates next to each. This will enable you to work on those that are the most important at any given time. At this point, you will need to identify what resources are required to achieve each of the goals (eg facilities, time, support staff). If these resources are not available, you may need to amend goals or re-prioritise.

STEP 3: Setting the targets (goals)

Having identified the most important qualities for success and estimated the performer's current standing on each quality, you can set a goal for improvement for each quality (remember to ensure the goals set are SMARTER).

STEP 4: Taking action

Now you must set out with your performers the action or strategy needed to bring about the desired improvement (eg training methods, learning mental skills, changes in lifestyle). Once agreed, this action must be carried out.

STEP 5: Monitoring and re-evaluating

This is very important. In addition to monitoring progress towards the goal continuously, you should reassess the performer's current status (in relation to this goal) after a previously agreed period of time. If the performer achieves or is close to achieving the goal, it was probably an appropriate goal. If the performer is still some way from achieving this target, you will need to discuss the reasons. If necessary, you may need to reset the goal at a more appropriate level or set some short-term goals as stepping stones to help him/her move towards the original goal.

Read the example in Table 3 over the page.

---

1   For further advice on the use of performance profiling, you are referred to the NCF **Performance Profiling** tape and booklet, available from Coachwise Ltd (0113 231 1310).

STEP 1: Analyse player needs
Current status: 75% success rate from the free throw line in competitions (training score is 85% in simulated competition conditions)
STEP 2: Determine priority
Coach and player discuss performance and agree the key factor in improving free throw success is the need to improve concentration. They agree a rating of 6/10 for concentration at the free throw line.
STEP 3: Set goals
Major goal: To achieve 95% success rate from the free throw line in simulated competitive situation by the end of July.

STEP 4: Take action

April	May	June	July
Use concentration drills in one session per week. Develop a free throw routine to aid concentration.	Use concentration drills and routine in free throw drills in one session a week.	Use concentration skills and routine in simulated competition situation in one training session a week.	Use concentration skills and routine in competitions, continue practise in training and include distractions.

STEP 5: Monitor and re-evaluate goal

	May		July
	Reassess free throw score in simulated competitive situation last week of May *Score 87%* *With player, reset goal to 90%*		Reassess free throw score in simulated competitive situation last week of July (may assess also in competition) *Score 91%* *Exceeded revised goal.*

Table 3: Example of the goal-setting process for a basketball player

NB Original goal was readjusted at the end of May as progress was not as rapid as anticipated. However, in exceeding revised goal at the end of July, player's confidence in his/her ability to perform at the free throw line should have increased.

Reviewing goals and giving feedback

Stage 5 is a very important part of the process, all too often forgotten or handled poorly. You will need to set time aside both to set agreed goals prior to training and to review goals and provide feedback after the session. Remember, the way feedback is provided is crucial, particularly if the goal has not been achieved. Confidence is often fragile and repeated failure will generally result in confidence being lost.

Guidelines for giving feedback

- First give the performer an opportunity to say how he/she feels. It may be a good rule to request the positive things first, then the things that went less well or badly. Give time to share feelings. This is important in helping the performer to accept responsibility for the outcome and learn to be analytical and objective rather than simply emotional.
- In adding your own feedback, follow a similar pattern – positives first, then negatives as necessary. Ensure any negative or corrective comments address performance or behaviour, not the person (eg 'I felt your performance lacked effort and commitment' rather than 'You were lazy'). Always try to end on a positive note and give the performer something constructive on which to work. As necessary, reassure and confirm your belief in his/her ability and commitment to his/her goals.
- Agree and reset goals as necessary.

Types of goal

You will probably find that some goals are based on:

- an outcome or performance level (collectively these are called **product goals**)
- a sub-component of performance (eg a specific aspect of a shot, such as the follow-through, approach or footwork, called a **process goal**).

Each of these types of goal can be beneficial to self-confidence under specific circumstances (Table 4 over the page).

Type of Goal	Definition	When Useful/Effect on Self-confidence
Outcome goals: (type of product goal)	Goals concerned with results (ie finishing position, win-loss)	May be ultimate goal but needs controllable sub-goals
Performance goals (type of product goal)	Goals relating to achieving an absolute standard (eg time, distance, height, personal improvement)	Can enhance long-term motivation, needs regular (positive) feedback
Process goals	Goals which focus attention on specific aspects of performance, those things which result in success	Assists learning, achievement provides valuable information on competence

Table 4: Types of goals and their potential influence on self-confidence

How it works

Dependent on the specific situation, the type of goal set and the disposition of the performer, effective goal-setting can therefore help to build confidence by:

- providing a measure of performance (ie information on current strengths and weaknesses)
- clarifying expectations
- focusing attention
- providing a challenge
- providing regular success
- increasing motivation to achieve
- ensuring regular and accurate feedback.

However, this will only happen if goals are set appropriately and the feedback provided regularly, accurately and in a positive and constructive way. You will have a chance to use goal-setting to build self-confidence in Part Two (Programme 2 Page 60).

2.2 Positive Thinking and Self-talk[1]

Coaches often use verbal persuasion (eg 'You can do it') to build confidence and this can be highly effective. However, if coaches are to empower their performers to have greater control over their own confidence levels, performers also need to develop their own techniques to boost confidence. Self-confidence is about believing in your own ability, so strategies that promote positive thinking and the use of positive statements about yourself can be extremely effective ways of promoting confidence. Some people seem to have a natural tendency to think positively – *they see the glass as half full.* Others tend to be more pessimistic – they dwell on the negatives, on doubts and tend to *see the glass as half empty.*

Half empty?

Half full?

Irrespective of these tendencies, most people indulge from time to time in some form of self-talk – a term used to describe what people say to themselves – either out loud or as a small voice inside their head. This self-talk tends to be either positive or negative (rarely neutral). Sports performers often demand perfection from themselves and can be very self critical when they fail to attain it. This negative self-talk can adversely affect subsequent performance in the manner shown in Figure 3.

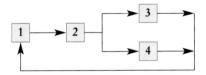

1 Negative appraisal of performance or current ability

2 Negative self-statements (and thoughts)

3 Reduced confidence in ability to achieve

4 Emotional and behavioural response (eg increased anxiety, avoiding particular situations)

Figure 3: Relationship between negative self-talk, performance and confidence

---

1   These are sometimes referred to as **affirmations.**

It is therefore as important to counter negative self-talk as it is to induce positive self-talk.

Figure 4: Examples of positive and negative self-talk

Positive self-talk is a powerful way through which performers can reinforce positive feelings, images and thoughts while lessening the effects of negative distractions. It is a skill which, once learned, can be used at any time – before, in and after both training and competition.

How positive are you? Do you typically see the glass as half empty or half full? Do you usually have positive or negative images of yourself? Do you find negative thoughts and statements slip into your consciousness? When? At the start of a challenging day? Before an important competition? During a competition – perhaps at a critical moment? Do you dwell on things that went wrong and relive negative thoughts and pictures?

From Figure 4, you can see that self-talk can be **task-related** (where the emphasis of the self-talk is on the task being attempted (eg 'I just can't pass the ball consistently to the left') or **emotion-related,** where the emotion associated with the experience is the focus of the statement (eg 'I'm so scared of failing in front of the rest of the team').

ACTIVITY 8

1 Write down typical negative self-statements or images you have experienced (in sport, work, relationships):

Typical Statements	T/E	Results

2 For each one, note whether they are task-related (T) or emotion-related (E) in the middle column.

3 Note what happens in the results column – what emotions you feel, what effects on behaviour or performance, what happens to your own confidence.

Now turn over.

Most people talk to themselves from time to time and these often express negative feelings or thoughts:

1 *Typically, you may dread certain situations (eg making presentations, playing in front of a large crowd) and experience all sorts of negative images and self-statements beforehand (eg 'I always get so nervous, I muddle up my words; I get distracted by the crowd and then everything goes wrong and I play badly'). Instead of concentrating on the **what needs to be done**, you focus on **what might go wrong** (the outcome).*

2 *Most people make self-statements that can relate to either the task (T) or an emotion (E) associated with it. The positive statements used to counter negative self-talk should match whichever type is being made (eg if you make a task-related negative statement, you should try to counter this with a positive task-related statement).*

3 *Perhaps you recognise certain situations during a competition when self doubts creep in and negative statements run through your head (eg at game point down in tennis – 'Don't let me serve a double fault now'; as you approach the bell in a 1500 metre race – 'I don't think I have enough left to make the break'). The negative words and images influence the selection and execution of the action – they seem to preset the system to produce the behaviour that matches the image and thought (ie the double fault, the lack of pace in the last lap).*

After an event, particularly one in which you were unsuccessful, you may focus on everything that failed to go to plan and overlook the things that went well. You condemn yourself for making the errors (eg 'How could I serve a double fault at match point? Why can I never run a fast last lap if I am ahead?'). These negative thoughts and statements dent your confidence and may be relived the next time similar events occur, so reinforcing the creation of negative images and thought patterns in the future.

Recognising negative self-talk

The first step is for the performer to **identify** the negative thoughts and statements and discover **when** they typically occur. Most performers are already aware of these or, through prompting at key moments (eg pressure situations), can begin to recognise them. You will have a chance to do this with your performers in Part Two (Programme 2 Page 60).

Turning negative to positive

Identifying situations where negative statements regularly occur is the first step in changing negative statements into positive self-talk that is more likely to elicit positive behaviours and so greater self-belief and confidence[1]. Try Activity 9.

---

1   In addition to translating negative into positive thoughts, it is also possible to use the technique of thought stopping to halt the negative thoughts from interfering with performance.

ACTIVITY 9

1   Read the following examples of negative statements often used in different sports and the sample positive alternatives:

Negative	Positive
I hate playing in the wind (eg before a tennis match)	Nobody likes the wind but I know how to cope with it
I hope I don't miss this one (eg before shot at target, before third long jump)	Deep breath and focus on the bull's eye I know I can do it right – smooth run, short steps, hit the board
He's fast – how will I cope? (eg rugby back, hockey defence)	Use my superior experience and skill to out-think him
I always have a poor start in this pool (swimming)	This pool's the same as any other. Just go on the starter.
I'm never very good at half time talks (time outs) when the game is not going well (eg netball, volleyball, basketball coach)	Keep it simple – stick to two key points

2   Write down your negative statements from Activity 8 and then turn each into a positive one that you feel would elicit a positive attitude/behaviour from you:

Negative	Positive

Now turn over.

Review your answers but remember that positive self-talk is most effective when:

- *the user (performer, coach) can associate with the phrase – it is personal to them*
- *it recreates strong feelings and images associated with a previously successful attempt (at the skill or task)*
- *it triggers appropriate action by reminding the performer/coach what to do*
- *it is brief and easy to remember.*

Self-talk is relatively easy to use – the most difficult part is to identify accurately the negative feelings and self-statements as they happen. This will improve with practice. Once performers have positive self-statements for use at the critical points in their sport, these can become part of the performance strategy (ie not waiting for negative thoughts to be recognised but using the self-talk whenever appropriate).

When should performers use self-talk?
To have the most beneficial effects, positive self-talk should be used in competition, especially at critical moments (eg before a big point, following a mistake). To develop this skill, performers need to practise using positive self-talk in training. Initially, specific techniques or drills can be isolated to allow the performer to develop the appropriate self-talk in specific situations. Simulated competition can then be used to allow performers to employ self-talk when appropriate. These progressive steps will pave the way to the effective use of self-talk in competition.

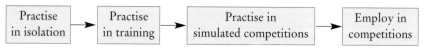

Figure 5: Stages in introducing self-talk

In addition, the more general use of positive statements to reinforce a positive self-image can be used to bolster confidence. The following examples might be used by performers:

Before training (perhaps kept in the kit bag):
> *I'm feeling strong – I'm going to train hard.*

Before a competition (perhaps pinned up in a prominent place):
> *I've put in the work in training – I know I can produce the goods today.*
> *I know my technique is sound after all that practice.*

After a competition:
> *I was disappointed with my performance today*
> *but I learnt a lot and it will pay off in the future.*

Remember that to be effective, positive self-talk should:

- focus the performer on the immediate task
- evoke strong positive emotions (eg a will to succeed)
- trigger appropriate action (eg the correct starting position)
- be brief and easy to remember.

2.3 Imagery

When faced with a challenging task (eg learning or changing a specific technique, using a new tactic), it often helps to see others perform it successfully, especially if they possess similar skills. How often have you heard children when attempting a difficult task say 'You go first... no, you go first'? This is probably because each wants to see someone else try the task first. This is especially the case when the task is new or perceived to be difficult.

Alternatively, if you have successfully achieved something in the past, watching a replay of it helps you believe you can do it again. If there is no video record, you can of course review it in your mind. This skill of visualising past (or future) performances is referred to as imagery[1].

---

[1] You may also find the terms **visualisation** and **mental rehearsal** used.

More than just pictures

Imagery involves creating a clear mental picture – of the venue, the performance, the conditions, the people. Often it relies most strongly on the visual image. This type of visual imagery can be created in two forms:

- **External imagery** where the performer sees the performance as if it was a video recording (ie through the eyes of an observer such as the coach).

- **Internal imagery** where the performer views the performance through his or her own eyes (ie as if actually performing).

In addition, some use can also be made of **association imagery** where the performer creates an image of something (eg an animal) which depicts the qualities he/she is trying to produce (eg to sprint like a tiger, to soar like a bird).

Each type of imagery can be beneficial for different purposes. It is generally accepted, however, that internal imagery is the most useful and perhaps the most powerful, as it encourages the simultaneous use of all the senses – hearing, feeling, smelling and tasting as well as seeing. For example, the cricket batsman might visualise seeing the flight of the ball in the air, feeling the position of the bat in the hand and the tension of the muscles in the arm, hearing the sound of the bat hit the ball and then watching the trajectory of the ball in the air or along the ground. Smell and taste may also add to the strength of the image. In fact, the more senses involved and the stronger the image, the more effective the imagery seems to be.

Sense	Example
Sight	Venue, conditions, equipment, opposition, movements, officials, spectators
Hearing	Sound of own breathing, opponent's calls, officials, spectators, equipment, coach
Touch/feeling	Feel of equipment, body sensations (muscle, joint, balance) associated with movement, warmth/rain/wind
Smell	Wet grass, leather ball, sea breeze, embrocation
Taste	Own sweat, gum shield, chlorinated water

Table 5: Examples of sensory input to imagery

How is it used?

Imagery can be used to simulate the actual execution of a technique or performance. This means that the body responds as if actually performing a technique (although the neuro-muscular sensations are less strong than with real performance), but with the added advantage of being able to change and repeat movements in ways that might be difficult if actually performing the task.

Imagery also allows performers to develop a mental blueprint of key movements and aspects of performance. By developing this blueprint, performers can better detect errors in their movements and so more effectively correct them. This process means that skills can be learned and mastered more quickly.

One of the benefits of imagery as a tool for building confidence is that it allows the performer to use all the senses to recreate the sensation of a previous (or future) good performance – a positive image of the good performance, of doing it right. It can be used at different times:

- When used before an event (ie days, hours or immediately before – instant **pre-play**), imagery can replace negative thoughts, reduce any effects of anxiety, rehearse the correct action or tactic and so raise confidence.

- Immediately prior to a situation (eg at the free throw line in basketball, on the blocks in a sprint event), it can also improve concentration and provide a form of mental **rehearsal** or practice of the actual execution of the perfect action.

- Imagery can also be used after an action **(replay).** If the action was successful, it can provide excellent feedback and reinforcement of good practice which will boost confidence[1].

A lack of confidence can lead to a hesitant performance, a loss of attentional focus and even a mental image of mistakes and failures. Imagery can also be used to practise different aspects of the skill, so increasing success (or the expectation of success) and bolstering confidence:

- It can be used to build confidence in interpreting cues correctly and making appropriate decisions. For example, cricket batsmen can use imagery to picture the incoming bowler, select the available cues (eg of hand position, line and length) to identify the type of ball to be delivered and rehearse the selection of the best response.

- Imagery can also be used to rehearse the correct action – the feel of the stroke, the sound of the ball on the bat, the flight of the ball from the bat. Similarly the gymnast might rehearse the vault – the run-up and flight onto the board; the flight on, touch and dismount from the horse. Perfect imagery not only rehearses the correct movement and focuses attention onto the key aspects of the action but it also builds confidence.

---

1   Imagery can also be used for other purposes such as to analyse performance, then identify errors, before using pre-play to replace the error with the perfect action.

- Imagery can also be used to replay the action to provide more extensive feedback – about both the correct and incorrect aspects of the performance. If the performer can quickly identify the error and replay the correct action, attention is focused on correct movements and a successful image is created and confidence restored.

How to learn

Many people (and indeed most top performers) use imagery but the important skill is to learn to use it systematically and regularly. To become proficient in using imagery, performers need to practise the techniques on a regular basis – first away from training. The evidence suggests that the more relaxed the individual, the more readily and vividly he/she is able to generate the images, sounds and feelings. If you are not very familiar with imagery, try the next activity.

ACTIVITY 10

1 Identify a task or skill from your own sport and describe a range of sensations associated with it. It might help to think of a specific occasion when you carried out this task or skill successfully:

- Sight:

- Hearing:

- Touch:

- Smell:

- Taste:

---

2 Read the following instructions carefully so you are familiar with them:

Preparation
Make yourself comfortable in a chair.

Exercise
- Take in a long slow breath, hold for a silent count of three, relax and breathe out slowly. Repeat twice and close your eyes.
- Think of a pleasant sporting occasion where you performed well. Run the image through your mind at normal speed until you reach the end or until your concentration wavers.
- Count from one to three and open your eyes.

2 Now try the exercise.

3 After the exercise, answer the following questions by circling the appropriate response(s):

- How vividly were you able to experience the event?　　　Very / Somewhat / Not very well / Not at all

- Which senses were you able to evoke?　　　Sight / Sound / Feel/touch / Smell

- Did you experience the events as though you were there – seeing, hearing and feeling everything through your own senses as it happened (ie using internal imagery)?　　　Yes / No

- Did you experience the events as if you were watching a film or video, like a recording of yourself carrying out the action (ie using external imagery)?　　　Yes / No

- Did you switch between the two types?　　　Yes / No

4 You may wish to repeat the exercise again.

NB Like any other skill, plenty of practice is needed to develop and hone the skill of imagery – short bursts (five to ten minute sessions) seem to be most effective.

The main advantage of imagery is that it allows performers to practise in any location at any time. In addition, once imagery is mastered, performers will be able to focus their imagery at specific points of performance when it is most needed (eg between points, during the warm-up, when things are not going well). Imagery can complement physical training by allowing the performer to attempt new techniques and reinforce successes. It can also allow practice during times of injury or illness. To be effective, however, imagery should be focused and used at appropriate times. Programme 4 in Part Two (Page 74) will help you to use imagery skills to build self-confidence.

Remember, imagery can be used to:

- pre-play   this can allow the performer to prepare and sense a successful performance
- replay   to analyse performance, identify strengths (and weaknesses)
- attempt new skills   for example, modelled on another's performance
- correct faults   in training and competition

2.4 Developing Routines

Sport is full of factors that cannot be controlled, such as weather conditions, unfavourable officiating calls, unlucky bounces, deflections and equipment failure. All these can increase uncertainty and affect confidence. Effective performers therefore plan their own success by focusing on the things they can control. Often they adopt an organised and consistent approach to their behaviour and performance – they pack their kit in the same way to ensure nothing is forgotten, they do the same warm-up, they go through the same ritual before they serve or take a free throw (eg bouncing the ball a certain number of times), before they go down on the blocks or prepare for the vault. They seem to have a well-learned, consistent routine they execute every time – in the same order, with the same timing.

It seems that if you have a consistent base from which to perform, you feel more confident, and maintain better control (eg over timing, concentration, emotions, if things go wrong). In addition, the familiarity means that limited attention needs to be given to routine tasks; they just happen without conscious effort and with less likelihood of things being forgotten. They are used in everyday life as well – for routine tasks (eg getting up in the morning, starting the car, locking the house, doing the shopping) as well as in potentially difficult situations (eg preparing to give a presentation, handling the morning of an examination or interview).

Routines can help to build or restore confidence by providing a positive focus, and a familiar and organised pattern of behaviour on which to carry out a task successfully. Routines are often used by basketball players at the free throw line, tennis players prior to serving, sprinters preparing to leave the blocks and gymnasts before each event. They can also be used to provide some structure in the 24 hour period before a big competition or simply to help performers get in the groove quickly at the start of an event.

ACTIVITY 11

1   Describe any routines you have (eg on competition day, before coaching, after coaching sessions):

2   Explain why you have these routines, whether or not they help, and how they help:

3   Identify occasions when you think your performers use routines:

4   Describe any situations where routines might have a negative effect on the performer's attitude and therefore their confidence:

Now turn over.

---

3   *Many performers use routines prior to competitions and specific events within the competition:*

- *In preparation for competitions, routines ensure much of the preparation goes on automatically, allowing the focus to be placed on important variables (eg weather conditions, tactics) rather than routine elements (eg packing kit, changing, physical warm-up). As this preparation is relatively unchanging (routine), performers are more likely to be comfortable with it and able to focus where needed. No matter what else is going on around them, they can be confident in their routine.*

- *Routines are typically used before executing closed or self paced skills (eg taking a penalty, serving, driving off the tee, getting onto the blocks).*

4   *An over-reliance on or obsessive dependence on a rigid routine might be detrimental if for some reason it cannot be executed – you have too little time to complete the full warm-up, you cannot wear the favoured colour kit, you cannot be last onto the pitch or the block.*

Routines must be appropriately structured if they are to be effective. They may involve:

- doing physical tasks in a particular order (eg always packing kit the same way and at the same time, showering before eating the pre-match meal, putting kit on in a particular order, wiping hands on socks before taking the basketball at the free-throw line)

- preparing mentally in a particular way (eg always working through a relaxation technique the night before major events, using imagery as part of your warm-up, mentally rehearsing tactics before the event).

Some performers use the countdown approach to routines prior to important competitions – they identify ten important stages in the 24 hour period before the start of the event or for the day of the event, as explained in the following panel.

Typical routine for swimmer

Night before

- Familiarisation with accommodation, pool environment, eating facility.
- Pool session (light, if in taper phase) with emphasis on starts and turns, racing techniques, pace work and long swim-down.
- Relaxation and massage.
- Meal, good carbohydrate and fluid intake.
- Relaxation and imagery session.
- Warm shower, good night's sleep.

Morning of event

10   Wake up, use positive self-talk and imagery of the race.

9   Good breakfast with plenty of fluids at least two hours before event.

8   Team meeting or personal time for relaxation.

7   Travel time (use of mental skills).

6   General warm-up including 15 minutes stretching work, 45–60 minutes swim.

5   Warm shower and change into dry warm clothes.

4   Structured time away from pool-side during which watch some events, observe the starter.

3   35–40 minutes before event prepare for race – 25 minute stretching/pulse raising with relaxation and imagery work working through race plan.

2   Ten minutes before start to pool side – goggles and hat on early, general focusing and relaxation, imagery of start and first turn.

1   To blocks – slowly remove outer clothing (often a routine to order) in last 30 seconds, sit on block or stand behind, focusing on lane and imagery of start and first turn, deep breathing to relax.

All these familiar routines create a certain comfort and reassurance that can contribute to self-confidence. However, performers should be wary of making routines for too many aspects of performance and becoming overly superstitious about having to play them through without alteration. They should always be ready and willing to react to changing circumstances (eg make tactical changes when necessary). The over-use of, or dependence on, routines can make performers less adaptable and may threaten confidence. The guidelines provided in Programme 4 in Part Two (Page 74) will help you and your performers make effective use of routines and avoid some of the potential risks.

2.5   Summary and Further Help

In this chapter you have been introduced to the four mental skills selected to build self-confidence: goal-setting, positive self-talk, imagery and routines. Each skill was introduced and examples provided to highlight the potential use to build self-confidence. In the next chapter, you will be encouraged to analyse the strengths and weaknesses of your performers so you can identify the most appropriate mental skills for each of them.

Further help on mental skills work, and in particular on these four mental skills, can be found in:

Sellars, C (1996) **Mental skills: an introduction for sports coaches.** Leeds, National Coaching Foundation. ISBN 0-947850-34-1.

Morris, T (1997) **Psychological skills training in sport: an overview.** (2nd edition) Leeds, National Coaching Foundation. ISBN 0-947850-78-3.

They are available from Coachwise Ltd (0113 231 1310).

Chapter Three: Profiling your Performer

3.0 What's in It for You?

Having considered the essential mental qualities for successful sports performance and some of the techniques that might be used to develop these qualities, you now need to identify the specific needs of your performers. What are their strengths and weaknesses? How confident are they? How might the needs of one performer differ from another?

In this chapter you will use the technique of performance profiling[1] to examine the factors that influence success in your sport and to assess your performer's strengths and weaknesses against this profile. Although the technique is used to profile every aspect of performance (physical, technical, tactical and mental), the emphasis will be placed on the mental factors (and particularly the role of self-confidence) and an evaluation of the extent to which your performers currently use mental skills. By the end of this chapter, you should be able to:

- profile the qualities needed to improve competitive performance in one of your athletes
- identify with your performer the mental skills needed to develop these essential qualities
- assess your performer's current use of selected mental skills and agree priorities
- use performance profiling to monitor the development of mental skills
- select which mental skills training programmes will be most suitable for your performer
- determine when you should embark on any form of mental skills work.

---

1 This is a technique developed by Richard Butler. If you are familiar with this technique, you may wish to skim this section. For further guidance on this technique, you are recommended to the NCF pack **Performance Profiling**, available from Coachwise Ltd (0113 231 1310).

3.1 How to Profile

Most coaches assess their performers' strengths and weaknesses but often in an *ad hoc* way and sometimes without keeping a record of these assessments. One more systematic method gaining popularity with coaches is that of performance profiling. This technique enables both the coach and performer to record their respective assessments of the performer's ability on each key aspect of performance.

ACTIVITY 12

1 In relation to one of your performers (Performer A), make a list of the ten factors that contribute most significantly to his/her performance level (it will help if you think of specific performances and consider technical/tactical, physical and mental factors). List these in the left-hand column (leave all the other columns blank):

Performer A	Rank	Performer B	Rank

2   Record what you notice about the qualities in your list:

- What is the balance in terms of physical, technical/tactical and mental factors?

- Which ones change over time?

- How many are controllable by you or your performer?

3   Focus on the mental qualities you listed and consider the following:

- How important is mental toughness – the four Cs in your list (confidence, concentration, control and commitment)?

- Did you mention confidence directly or indirectly? Do you think this should be in your list?

- Note any other observations:

4   If necessary, go back and amend the qualities listed in Question 1.

Now turn over.

You have now started the profiling process.

1   *You might like to compare your factors with the qualities you generated in Activity 1 in the first chapter (Page 2).*

2   *You may wish to reflect on the relative importance given to mental factors in relation to physical and technical/tactical ones. How different might the factors be in relation to another performer?*

If your list consisted of predominantly controllable factors (those that can be influenced by you or your performer), then you will be able to adapt your coaching sessions to bring about suitable changes. If your list was full of uncontrollable factors (eg the weather, opponents), you and your performer may become demoralised and lose confidence with your inability to bring about change (when required).

If your list has more than five uncontrollable factors, go back and check if you omitted any controllable factors that had a significant influence.

3   *Confidence may well have appeared on your list, for most performers suffer fluctuations in self-confidence. If it did, you can be sure that this person's performance will benefit from improved or maintained self-confidence. However, even if self-confidence did not appear directly, it will inevitably have influenced some of the factors you listed. Go back to your list in Question 1 and underline the factors influenced by self-confidence.*

Performance profiling will help you and your performer identify the most important influences on performance. By doing this, you will be able to prioritise areas on which to work and therefore better inform your coaching programmes (eg your prioritisation will help determine long and short-term objectives). A performer's profile is, however, very individual. To contrast the similarities and differences, try the next activity.

ACTIVITY 13

1   Repeat Activity 12 for another of your performers (Performer B) and record the factors in the third column on Page 44.

2   For each performer, now rank the relative importance of the ten factors using the column marked rank (ie if power is deemed the most important, rank it as 1, if concentration is the next most important, rank it as 2, and so on).
     NB Even if some of the qualities are the same, the ranking for each performer may be different.

3   Contrast your two lists and summarise the similarities and differences:

4   Note the relative importance of confidence:

Now turn over.

You probably found that even if your lists contained many similar factors, they may have been ranked quite differently. This is perfectly natural but does highlight the importance of treating each performer as an individual. If the key factors that influence two performers are ranked differently, this may need to be reflected in the training programme and the coaching methods used. It may be only after such an exercise that these differences are apparent (to you and your performers).

Having looked more closely at the factors or qualities that influence success for each of your performers and perhaps focused more clearly on mental qualities, you should discuss these with your performers – their thoughts on the most significant ten qualities and their relative importance to success. You will have a chance to do this in Part Two (Programme 1 Page 54).

3.2 Why Profile?

Performance profiling is an excellent technique to help coaches and performers to:

- identify the important components of performance
- clarify and agree training and competition priorities
- set goals
- monitor the success of their coaching.

To be effective, ensure you observe the following guidelines.

Guidelines for using performance profiling

- Use performance profiling to identify and record your own and your performer's targets for mental skills training.
- Agree with your performer his/her current level of performance at key mental skills.
- Use the performance profiling process to form the basis of long- and medium-term goal-setting.
- Performance profiling can be used as part of your ongoing monitoring of mental skills (do not over-use).

3.3 When to Profile

Be careful you do not misuse performance profiling by using it too often. An example of the frequency of profiling is shown in Figure 6 (although this will vary according to your needs).

Month	J	F	M	A	M	J	J	A	S	O	N	D
Phase	Competitive season				Rest	Pre-season			Early competitive season			
Profile		✔				1st ✔			✔			✔

Figure 6: Example of profiling frequency (rugby union)

ACTIVITY 14

Now complete a similar chart for your sport. Mark on the chart the phases of your competitive year. Indicate when in the year you will profile your performer (this will need to be flexible as circumstances may change):

Month	J	F	M	A	M	J	J	A	S	O	N	D
Phase												
Profile												

NB You may wish to refer back to Activity 3 on Page 10 where you identified when mental skills training would be introduced into your training programme.

Programme 1 in Part Two (Page 54) should be completed at the point identified in Activity 14 as most appropriate for initial profiling.

3.4 Your Performer

Before embarking on the programmes in Part Two, you should reflect on the confidence levels of your performers and the mental skills they may currently employ (consciously or largely unconsciously). The next activity may be helpful.

ACTIVITY 15

Answer the following questions about your performer (if you intend to work with more than one performer, you will either need to use a different coloured pen or photocopy this activity):

1   I would rate my performer's general
    tendency to be self-confident in
    training situations as: High / Good / Unstable / Poor / Low

    I would rate my performer's general
    tendency to be self-confident in
    competitions as: High / Good / Unstable / Poor / Low

2   You may wish to ask your performers to rate their attitude towards a
    particular situation (eg a particular training session or element; a competition)
    – either by placing a mark on a scale such as:

    very positive   very negative
    and confident   and worried

    or by using faces such as:

3   You might rate your performer's ability to use different mental skills by
    completing the following:

    My performer can use:

    •   goal-setting   Very well / Quite well / Somewhat / A little / Not at all
    •   positive self-talk   Very well / Quite well / Somewhat / A little / Not at all
    •   imagery   Very well / Quite well / Somewhat / A little / Not at all
    •   routines   Very well / Quite well / Somewhat / A little / Not at all

4   My performer uses:

    •   goal-setting   Always / Frequently / Sometimes / Rarely / Never
    •   positive self-talk   Always / Frequently / Sometimes / Rarely / Never
    •   imagery   Always / Frequently / Sometimes / Rarely / Never
    •   routines   Always / Frequently / Sometimes / Rarely / Never

You will have a further chance to check this out in Programme 1 (Page 54).

3.5 Summary and Further Help

In this chapter you have been introduced to performance profiling as a technique to help you identify with your performers their relative strengths and weaknesses and so help you to prioritise training needs and set appropriate goals. You have used this technique to identify significant performance qualities and identify one quality which, when improved, will positively influence self-confidence. The means by which this quality can be improved is the subject of the remainder of this pack. You may already have decided that certain mental skills seem more appropriate for your needs than others.

If you wish to know more about the technique of profiling, you are strongly encouraged to read one or more of the following:

Butler, R (1996) **Performance profiling** (tape and booklet) Leeds, National Coaching Foundation. ISBN 0-947850-36-8.

Sellars, C (1966) **Mental skills: an introduction for sports coaches.** Leeds, National Coaching Foundation. ISBN 0-947850-34-1.

They are available from Coachwise Ltd (0113 231 1310).

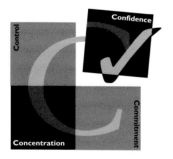

Mental Skills Programmes

Introduction

There are six mental skills programmes in Part Two. You may already have decided which mental skills seem most appropriate for your performers. However, you are strongly advised to complete Programme 1 on performance profiling over the page before embarking on any other programme offered in this pack. You should then be able to select:

- which programmes might be most suitable for your performer

- when you should embark on any form of mental skills work.

You are then invited to choose any programme, introduce the technique and evaluate its use. You may find that after using a given technique, you or your performer would benefit from one or more of the others. If so, use the programmes as you feel appropriate. Alternatively, you may wish to offer guidance on all the techniques and allow performers to decide with which they feel most comfortable. These can then be developed individually.

Whichever method you use, the programmes will progress through similar stages:

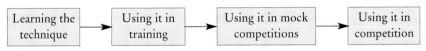

Figure 7: Mental skills programmes

Help will also be given on ways to monitor and evaluate its relative value to performers.

Programme One: Profiling your Performer

AIM

To help coaches and performers use performance profiling to identify the qualities needed to increase confidence.

In Activity 12 (Page 44), you were encouraged to draw up the ten most important factors for success for two specific performers you coach. In this programme, you will develop this further working with your performer(s) to build up a profile and identify the quality which, with improvement, will contribute most to self-confidence.

By the end of this programme, you should be able to use profiling to:

- identify the quality which, with improvement, would result in a significant rise in self-confidence

- determine the amount of improvement required to increase the performer's feelings of self-confidence in the short/medium term (within two to three months).

In this programme, you will need to work with your performers on one occasion outside coaching for between one and two hours.

Outside coaching session (1–2 hours)

Ask your performers to write down the ten most important qualities they feel contribute to their success in sport. Discuss these qualities with them and share your ideas (from Activity 12). You will need to come to some consensus about the ten. Try to establish what exactly your performer means by each quality (it may be different from your meaning).

Quality (Generated by Performer)	Description of Quality (by Performer)
Example from tennis: concentration in tight situations	Focusing on the right tactics in critical situations (eg at game points and tie-breaks)

Keep this record of the meaning of these significant qualities – you will need to refer back to it later.

2 Using these qualities as labels, complete the outer ring of the profile in Figure 8 (if you have less than ten labels, you can leave some blank or agree additional labels to add).

Figure 8:
Profile of
your performer[1]

3 Agree with your performer the ideal score (out of ten) on each of these qualities (ie identify the ultimate goal for this performer). Look first at Figure 9.

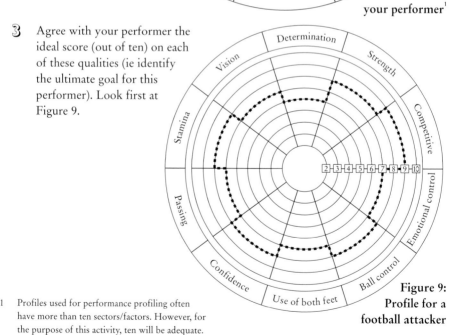

Figure 9:
Profile for a
football attacker

1   Profiles used for performance profiling often have more than ten sectors/factors. However, for the purpose of this activity, ten will be adequate.
NB Before writing, you may wish to photocopy this profile for future use.

4   Mark your agreed ideal scores for this performer on your profile in Figure 8.

5   For each of the qualities in your profile, agree your performer's current level and mark these in a different colour on your profile (your performer should lead this part of the profiling as it is his/her perceptions of competence that will significantly influence self-confidence level).

6   The difference between these two sets of scores identifies the improvements needed in each of the qualities[1]. For each of your qualities, record the difference between the two scores (ideal and current) in the following chart:

Qualities	Ideal score	Current score	Difference

1   For more detail on how to use performance profiling, you are referred to the NCF **Performance Profiling** pack.

7 Ask the performer to select the quality that if improved would make a significant difference to his/her feelings of self-confidence (eg if I could improve my speed, I would feel a lot more confident). You, as coach, may need to help and negotiate here to identify a quality that:

- you believe the performer can improve over the next two to three months (so the purpose of the mental skill programmes in this booklet can be achieved)
- would be an appropriate focus for training over the next two to three months (ie in relation to the training programme, competitions, other goals)
- would result in increased confidence.

8 Agree with your performer how much improvement would be required to result in increased feelings of confidence (eg if currently a 6, will achieving a 7 suffice?). Check it is challenging but attainable; then complete the following form[1].

Name:		Date:	
Quality selected:			Current rating:
Ideal score:	Improvement agreed:		Over time frame of:

9 You may wish to profile your performer's current experience and use of the mental skills used in this pack to help increase confidence. If so, draw up a profile of mental qualities and skills, and encourage your performer to add any additional labels.

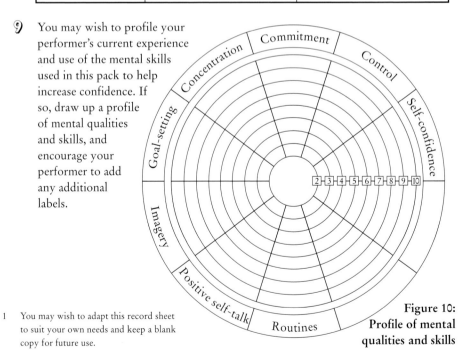

Figure 10: Profile of mental qualities and skills

1 You may wish to adapt this record sheet to suit your own needs and keep a blank copy for future use.

⏸️⓪ As before, agree the ideal score, current score and the differential between the two. This will help you to select suitable programmes from which your performer might benefit.

Qualities	Ideal score	Current score	Difference

Programme Two: Improving Self-confidence through Goal-setting

AIM

To help coaches and performers use goal-setting to improve self-confidence.

The judicious setting of goals (for any aspect of performance) not only provides a planning framework to help performers achieve their goals, it is also a means through which the performer can experience regular success. This success reinforces feelings of personal competency and so builds confidence.

Before embarking on this programme, ensure you are familiar with the principles of effective goal-setting, how goals can be set to build self-confidence (Chapter Two, Page 16) and have completed the performer profile from Programme One. By the end of this goal-setting programme, you should be able to:

- help performers set appropriate short, medium and long-term goals to achieve significant performance objectives

- monitor and adjust goals to enhance self-confidence

- provide meaningful feedback that promotes self-confidence

- help performers set appropriate competition goals to achieve success.

In this programme, you will need to work with your performers through a number of phases, some of which will span several occasions:

Phase A: *One session outside coaching session time (allow one to two hours).*

Phase B: *Over a number of coaching sessions (number and time frame dependent on action steps agreed).*

Phase C: *One session outside coaching session time (allow one to two hours).*

Phase D: *One occasion prior to competition.*

Phase A: One session outside coaching session time (allow one to two hours)

In Programme One (Page 54) you and your performer selected the quality which, when improved, would be most likely to enhance self-confidence. Work with your performer to discuss and agree the following:

For this quality and the target level to achieve in three months, identify with your performer goals for the following periods of time (first column over the page), together with the appropriate action required to achieve each goal (second column). The specific action (or strategy to achieve the goal) may involve gains in some aspect of fitness, improvements to an existing skill, the development of a new skill or tactic, or work on a specific mental quality (an example is provided in Table 6). Accomplishment will improve feelings of personal competence and so improve confidence.

Goals For	Action Required
Three months: To achieve an agreed concentration score through a whole match.	To use self-report measures of concentration after every match. Develop strategies to cope with various distractions in competition and record concentration scores.
One month: To maintain agreed concentration score at specific times of distraction (eg following an official's unfavourable decision, following a mistake) in training or a simulated competition.	Use specific training sessions to develop strategies to cope with particular distractions and record concentration scores. Introduce and practise using self-report measure of concentration (eg 10 point scale).
One week: To design and implement a distraction training session.	Prioritise identified distractions and develop a training session to develop concentration skills.
Next session: To identify specific occasions when distraction occurs.	Use recall and observation methods to identify specific distractions.

Table 6: Example of goals and required actions

Goals For	Action Required
Three months:	
One month:	
One week:	
Next session:	

These goals will provide specific markers against which both you and your performer can assess progress. Check your goals are SMARTER goals and ensure you have used the most appropriate type of goal (ie outcome, performance or process – refer back to Table 4 Page 26 if helpful), for each situation.

2   List the factors that most strongly influence the achievement of these goals:

•

•

•

3   If you have agreed appropriate goals with your performer, he/she should feel as though the programme for the next three months is challenging but realistic, and that with effort, a satisfying goal can be achieved. How challenging are these goals? For each of your goals identified in the previous table, ask your performer to rate how challenging they are at this moment (you may wish to do the same).

Goals	Degree of challenge		
Three months	Too low Challenging Too high 1 2 3 4 5		
One month	Too low Challenging Too high 1 2 3 4 5		
One week	Too low Challenging Too high 1 2 3 4 5		
Next session	Too low Challenging Too high 1 2 3 4 5		

NB It is only by achieving challenging goals that self-confidence will be enhanced: achieving unchallenging goals does not increase feelings of personal ability or progress, the likelihood is that goals that are too challenging will not be achieved. Check that all the goals you have agreed are appropriately challenging to your performer.

You may find it helpful to assess your performer's feelings of being challenged by his/her goals each week. If the degree of challenge changes, this may suggest the need to renegotiate the goal.

How confident are you that your performer will achieve these goals? You too should feel the goals are achievable with effort (if not, you and your performer may need to re-discuss and agree each of the goals). Inevitably your performer will experience periods of heightened self-confidence (eg following rapid improvement in training, after a successful competition) and phases of self-doubt (eg after a poor session or competition, during times of injury or illness). Indeed, self-confidence can alter from day to day. This is a normal part of sports participation. Your role is to help the performer maintain high confidence levels and make appropriate adjustments whenever confidence is low (or falling).

Phase B: Work with your performer in a normal coaching session to carry out the action plan and evaluate self-confidence.

Your performers should approach all training sessions confident both in their ability to achieve the goal for the session and that this will contribute to improved competition performance.

Immediately before the next training/coaching session, ask your performer to self-evaluate his/her self-confidence (use the first part of the form over the page; the second part should be used after the session to help monitor progress. NB you may wish to alter the design of this sheet to meet specific needs.)

Confidence Evaluation Form[1] (to complete prior to the session)		
Goal for the session:		
Degree of challenge in this goal:	Too low Challenging Too high 1 2 3 4 5	
How confident are you of achieving this goal?	Very positive Very negative and confident and unconfident 5 4 3 2 1	
Action required to achieve goal (including resources):		
Time-scale:		
(to complete after the session)		
Degree to which goal achieved:	Goal fully achieved Goal not achieved 5 4 3 2 1	
Goal progression (next goal):		

2   What do you do if your performer's confidence before a session is low? If your performer rated his/her self-confidence as low, you may need to agree a different goal or introduce a process goal (if your current goal is a product goal). For example, if the goal was to introduce concentration skills during the session, and the performer rated confidence (in relation to this goal) as relatively low, you may agree with your performer to identify one aspect of performance where concentration is a key issue and set a goal to use a specific concentration technique on every relevant occasion (refer back to the basketball example on Page 24).

If self-confidence was assessed as low, write in the space provided a summary of your discussions and any changes to this performer's session goal:

[1] You may wish to photocopy this before using it.

3 If your performer scored **challenge** and **self-confidence** appropriately, conduct this session and, on completion, ask your performer to complete the remaining section of the Confidence Evaluation Form.

4 The importance of reviewing goals and providing feedback has already been stressed (refer back to Section 2.1 on Page 17). Examine your monitoring sheet. If you and your performer feel the session goal was achieved, you will want to set a new goal. If your performer (or you) feel the goal was not achieved, you may wish to discuss why it was not (eg was it due to controllable or uncontrollable factors) and determine how best to progress towards the goal (eg by modifying the conditions, adding process goals). Whatever you agree, your performer should feel as though he/she gained something from the session and has a challenging goal that will help progress.

Write your action plan in this space:

Phase C: Work with your performer outside normal coaching session time

After an appropriate period of time (eg several coaching sessions), you and your performer should re-assess progress towards the main goal (and possibly other goals identified in the profile). Discrepancies between the new current level and the target level should provide invaluable information on progress. You can use this information to evaluate the effectiveness of the action plan.

New Current Level on your Chosen Quality	Target level	Discrepancy

Summarise the effectiveness of your performer's action plan and any changes:

Phase D: Work with your performer to agree and evaluate a competition goal

Goal-setting can be used at almost every point in the training and competition programme. However, it is best not to overload your performers (or yourself) with too many goals at any one time, as this could cause confusion and anxiety. For example in competition, your performer might have one goal for each major aspect of performance but not more than two or three in total. Examples are provided in Table 7 to provoke thought. Remember, goals will be most effective when the performer feels he/she has ownership of them.

When?	Examples
Day before competition	Use a relaxation technique the night before competition. Use imagery to rehearse competition plan. Carry out a predetermined routine.
Pre-event goals	Arrive at the venue a set time before competition. Eat a predetermined meal a set time before warm-up. Check equipment/kit before leaving the house/hotel.
Warm-up goals	Use a predetermined warm-up routine every time. Use concentration techniques to focus on key aspects. Recite competition goals during the warm-up.
Competition goals	Use appropriate mental skills (eg routines) at agreed times. Use a specific tactic/plan. Ensure suitable liquids are taken at agreed times (eg half-time, between events).
Post-competition goals	Analyse performance with the coach the day after competition (ie not on competition day). Use imagery to replay the competition and correct errors. Refuel (take set amount of carbohydrate) within two hours of competition.

Table 7: Example competition goals

Before agreeing a goal for competition, you should note that goals that are appropriately challenging in training can become too difficult in competition (due to the various added pressures associated with competition). Remember too that if the goal is perceived by the performer to be too difficult, he/she will either not accept the goal or will become less confident of achieving it. Therefore, you should always agree the competition goal with your performer and be prepared to modify it if it appears that he/she is losing confidence in its achievement.

Carry out the following steps with your performer:

1 In relation to the quality identified to raise self-confidence, agree a competition goal.

2 Identify any action that might be needed to ensure the goal is achieved (eg the appropriate mental skills have been perfected in training, time has been put aside to evaluate the competition goal). Complete the box provided.

Quality/attribute:

Competition goal:

Action (before and/or after competition):

3 Having agreed your performer's competition goal (and ensured this is appropriately challenging, see Pages 18 and 66), this should be used in a competition.

4 Following the competition, you and your performer should evaluate goal achievement (remember, you may regard the degree of goal achievement differently).

You may wish to consider the following points when evaluating competition goals:

- What was the original competition goal(s)?
- What were the major influences on achieving this goal?
- Which of these influences were controllable (by you, the performer)?
- To what degree was the goal achieved?
- What were the main reasons for this level of goal-achievement?
- What will you/your performer do differently for the next competition?

Evaluate the effectiveness of your performer's competition goal here:

You and your performer may wish to set more than one competition goal. If so, repeat this process for each goal (but remember, do not over-complicate the competition or confuse your performer by setting too many goals – set no more than two to three key competition goals).

Recap
You might find the following checklist useful when setting goals:

Questions to ask yourself

- Do my performers know what their goals are and why we agreed them?
- Are the goals set based on an assessment of individual needs?
- Are my performer's existing goals broken down into intermediate and short-term goals?
- Have the goals been recorded (by coach and/or performer)?
- How will I monitor and evaluate goal-achievement?
- Have we agreed goals for the next training session and/or competition? If so:
  - how many goals did we agree?
  - are these goals for the key aspects of performance?
  - are they SMARTER goals?
- Are there other areas of performance or preparation that would benefit from goal-setting?

Programme Three: Improving Self-confidence through Self-talk

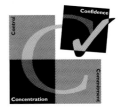

AIM

To help performers use positive self-talk to improve their self-confidence.

At some point most performers experience nagging doubts about their ability or a future event. These doubts are often associated with negative self-talk and can undermine feelings of self-esteem and confidence, as well as interfere with performance. Performers benefit from having techniques that allow them to focus on the positive by recognising and removing negative thoughts and replacing them with positive ones. One such technique is the use of positive self-talk.

Before embarking on this programme, ensure you have read the section on self-talk in Chapter Two (Page 27). If you have worked through Programme 2 on goal-setting, you may wish to incorporate this work into that action plan.

By the end of this programme, you should be able to:

- help performers identify their own negative self-talk
- turn negative into positive self-talk
- assess your performer's ability to use positive self-talk
- help performers use positive self-talk to enhance their self-confidence in training and competition.

In this programme, you will need to work with your performers on several occasions:

Phase A: One session outside coaching session time (allow one to two hours).

Phase B: Over a number of coaching sessions (number and time-frame dependent on action agreed).

Phase C: Introduce and use in competition.

Phase A: Work with your performer outside normal coaching session time (one to two hours)

꠸ Generate a list of self-statements used by one of your performers in the second column on the sample log page provided. This list can be generated in a number of ways:

- By asking performers to recall comments that typically come into their head at specified times (eg the night before a big competition, in preparation such as during the warm-up, at critical moments) during the competition/in training.

- By observing the performer in competition and training and noting occasions when self-talk seems to be occurring (eg it might be said out loud), behaviour might indicate negative thoughts. At a follow-up discussion with the performer, your observations might help to trigger recall on comments made or situations when self-talk is taking place and so help the performer recall actual words or thoughts.

- You might try to simulate situations in training that place the performer under pressure and so trigger self-talk. Words and thoughts can then be recorded.

Note when the statements are typically made in the first column (ie the situation such as at game point down, when going to the free throw line, when going onto the blocks), and whether the statement is positive (+) or negative (-). Leave the right hand column blank for the moment.

Sample log page

Situation	Self-talk	+ / -	Positive Self-talk

2 With your performer, change the negative statements into positive ones (refer back to Page 31 for further help if required) and write these in the right hand column. This may be achieved either by replacing the negative self-talk with the self-talk used when successfully achieving a goal or by rewording the negative phrases into a positive statement. Remember:

- it is important to ensure the phrase is personal to the performer (ie one with which he/she can associate)

- self-talk will be most effective when it recreates feelings and images associated with a previously successful attempt (at the skill or task) and reminds the performer of what to do next

- it is important to work through the process with performers so they understand why and how they can rephrase self-statements.

3 With each performer, select one situation and one negative self-statement – perhaps the one that occurs most regularly first or the one in which a lack of self-confidence is most damaging. Develop a plan to use this positive self-statement in subsequent training session/s. This will include when and how to use them. Look at Table 8 which shows an example from soccer and then complete your own sheet.

Occasion	Positive self-talk	Action
Before opposing free kicks within striking range	Use my vision	To direct the defence, correct own positioning, bounce on toes
During breaks in the action	Come on, keep sharp	To remember to stretch and jog to keep alert
Before goal kicks	Look for space	To check position of forwards and defenders (seek gaps)

Table 8: Example of self-talk from soccer

Your performer may wish to repeat this exercise in order to develop a number of key self-statements for use at different occasions.

4 Encourage the performer to rehearse using the positive statement. It may help to write it down on a card and place it somewhere prominent (eg on the mirror, in the kit bag, on the training log). If the performer is able to use imagery (Programme Four, Page 74), it will also help to rehearse the situation and visualise using the new positive self-statement and then enjoying the positive effect on subsequent performance.

Phase B: Over a number of coaching sessions

1 Design subsequent training sessions to ensure the performer has plenty of opportunities to try stopping the negative self-talk and replacing it with the positive statement.

2 Before each session, remind the performer and set a specific goal to use the statement in the session.

3 During the session, help the performer to remember to use it and afterwards, record how well it worked in the performer's log book. Note:

- how often the statement was remembered and used
- its effect on subsequent performance
- its effect on self-confidence.

Note:

- Be prepared to modify the statement if it does not seem to work.
- It may help to use thought stopping (example provided in Table 9) to break the negative thought pattern initially and trigger the reminder of the positive self-statement.

Negative Self-statement	Thought Stopping	Positive Self-statement
I bet I serve a double	Stop	Keep it simple and smooth, three quarter pace
I can't ski at all today	Change	I am a good skier – relax your knees and let it go

Table 9: Thought stopping examples

Try working through the same process using other negative self-talk in different situations and replacing it with appropriate positive self-statements.

Phase C: Introduce and use in competition

In this phase, your performer starts to use positive self-talk in simulated competitive situations and then in competition.

1 Set up a training session which best simulates competition. Use the checklist to ensure key considerations have been made (add your own considerations which may be peculiar to your sport).

Considerations	Comments
Opposition	
How can you make the training situation simulate future competition?	
Venue	
How similar is the venue to the future competitive venue?	
How can I build in typical distractions faced in competition?	
Importance	
Has the importance of the session been made clear to the performers?	

Ask your performer to use the positive self-statements (devised on Page 71) that have been practised in training sessions at appropriate points during the simulated competition. Encourage your performer to recite the self-statements out loud as they are used. This will help condition your performer to use self-statements whenever appropriate.

Recap
You might find the following checklist useful when using positive self-talk.

Questions to ask yourself:
- In what situations do performers tend to self-talk (positively and negatively)?
- What sort of things do they say on each occasion?
- Can performers turn their negative self-talk into positive self-talk?
- How can I help?
- Are there key positive phrases or words which performers can use to raise self-confidence?
- When might they use them?

Programme Four: Building Self-confidence Using Imagery

AIM

To help performers use imagery to enhance their self-confidence.

Imagery can help performers create or recreate the sensations associated with good performance and can therefore help performers believe in themselves and their own ability. Imagery can raise self-confidence in a number of ways. For example, performers can:

- use imagery to recall previous successful performances, reminding themselves of what it looks and feels like

- use imagery in warm-ups to pre-play what they must do next

- image various situations and rehearse how they cope with each

- image a role-model coping with situations that are new to them

- use imagery to rerun and correct previously difficult techniques.

Before embarking on this programme, ensure you have read the section on imagery in Chapter Two (Page 33).

By the end of this programme, you should be able to:

- devise practices to help performers develop their imagery skills

- design imagery scripts with your performers to increase self-confidence

- evaluate your performer's use of imagery and its effect on self-confidence.

In this programme, you will need to work with your performers on several occasions in different situations:

Phase A: With or without you but away from the sport situation.

Phase B: One session immediately following a coaching session in which they performed well (allow one to two hours).

Phase C: Over a number of coaching sessions (number and time-frame dependent on action agreed).

Phase D: Introduce and use imagery in competition.

Phase A: Away from the sport situation

] If your performer has little or no experience of using imagery, you may choose to introduce it away from the sport situation. You might suggest using a commercial tape to develop the basic skills or alternatively exercises to work through alone (you may need to adapt this to meet the specific nature of their training venue). An example is provided. Ensure you discuss the experience with your performer:

Introductory imagery exercise for a performer

Preparation: Read the following instructions carefully before trying the exercise:

- Make yourself comfortable in a chair.
- Take in a long slow breath, hold for a silent count of three, relax and breathe out slowly. Repeat twice and close your eyes.
- Think of the venue where you train and try to picture everything about it – the ground or floor, the trees, the walls if it takes place inside, your coach or trainer, any equipment you use, the clothes you wear, other performers.
- Try to hear the typical sounds – perhaps the sound of voices, of equipment; move around.
- Try to feel things – the feel of your own clothing, the feel of the ground under your feet or the water around you, the feel of the equipment.
- Run the image through your mind until your concentration wavers.
- Count from one to three and open your eyes.

NB It helps if you are relaxed[1] when you do this exercise so you might choose to sit in an easy chair, somewhere where you won't be disturbed; or even as you lie in the bath or in bed. You will probably need to read the ideas several times.

When you are familiar with the instructions, try the exercise.

---

[1] You may also wish to learn to use relaxation techniques.

2 After the exercise, use the following report form to monitor the effectiveness of the imagery[1].

Imagery report form

- How vividly were you able
  to experience the event?　　　　Very / Somewhat / Not very well / Not at all
- Which senses were you able to evoke?
  (circle more than one if appropriate)　　Sight / Sound / Feel & touch / Smell
- Did you experience the events as though you were there –
  seeing, hearing and feeling everything as it happened?　　　　　　Yes / No
- Did you experience the events as if you were watching
  a film or video?　　　　　　　　　　　　　　　　　　　　　　　Yes / No

Phase B: Work with your performer directly following a coaching session in which success was experienced (remember success may not necessarily mean winning)

1 During the session, try to observe as carefully as possible, everything you can that seems to accompany a successful action (a move, a stroke, a game) – such as facial expressions, body position, body language, any verbal comment, apparent focus.

2 After the session, ask the performer to recall everything about the successful action – they may quite quickly recall a number of things so be ready to jot them down – use exactly the same words.

3 Encourage them to try to use imagery to picture the scene again and then ask him/her to tell you everything seen, heard or felt. Check whether the performer was using internal (through own eyes) or external (like a video) visual imagery.

4 Together try to draw up as detailed and vivid a description as possible (use the chart on Page 77 if helpful). You may wish to prompt the performer by suggesting some of the things you observed but ensure it is the performer's image, not yours.

---

1 Once the performer has become more experienced in using imagery, you may wish to use a more comprehensive imagery evaluation– see Page 80.

Action (technique, movement):

I saw:

-
-
-

I heard:

-
-
-

I felt:

-
-
-

5 Ask the performer to image the whole scene – what they saw, heard and felt when they were successfully executing the action. Afterwards ask how vividly he/she was able to use each sense and which sense was the most powerful. Complete the following report:

- Was the imagery internal, external or did you switch from one to the other?

- How vividly did you see
  your images?   Not at all   1   2   3   4   5   Very vividly

- How clearly did you hear
  any sounds?   Not at all   1   2   3   4   5   Very clearly

- How vividly did you feel
  sensations associated with
  body movement?   Not at all   1   2   3   4   5   Very vividly

- How aware were you of
  your emotions during the
  imagery practice?   Not at all   1   2   3   4   5   Very aware

- How vividly were you able
  to detect smells?   Not at all   1   2   3   4   5   Very vividly

- How easily were you able to
  control your imagery?   Not at all   1   2   3   4   5   Very easily

- Which was the most powerful
  sense?   Sight / Sound / Feel & touch / Smell

---

6 Encourage the performer to practise the imagery away from the coaching environment, trying to utilise as many senses as possible to create a vivid image (this can be done by agreeing personal imagery goals with each performer, including using imagery away from training, before and after training/competition). You may wish to repeat this exercise with this performer on a number of occasions, encouraging him/her to be as descriptive as possible. The vividness questionnaire will help you monitor your performer's improvement.

Phase C: With your performer over a number of coaching sessions

1   Encourage the performer to use the imagery of a successful performance just prior to coaching sessions – you may need to allow extra time to do this. Your performer should now start to control his/her imagery. If the images start to vary from the original images, your performer should stop and try to recall the original sensations (associated with a successful attempt). Use the following guidelines[1].

Imagery Guidelines for Performers

- Immediately before the coaching session, find a quiet, safe place to practise your imagery.

- Sit or lie down and use a breathing exercise to evoke relaxation (eg count slowly 3-2-1, taking in a deep breath and exhaling slowly on each count).

- Either with your eyes open or shut (whichever you prefer), see yourself (external perspective) about to perform your chosen technique.

- Notice the surroundings, what you see, hear and smell.

- When you are ready, start to imagine successfully performing your technique, noticing as you do the sensations you have previously described. Try to make the speed of the images as close to the real time as possible.

- Now move into yourself, seeing and feeling the actions from within your body.

- If your images start to wander or you begin to imagine something else, refocus on the required task (it is essential to gain control over your imagery).

- Successfully complete the practice, making a mental note of all that you see, feel, hear and smell (including the quality and vividness of each sense).

- Now count to three and go to your coaching session, confident in your ability to perform the skill.

---

2   The guidelines may also form the basis of an imagery script and you may wish to record them onto an audio tape, perhaps with some favourite music which is calming and focusing. This might then be used to encourage practice at other times (eg before leaving home for training, before starting the warm-up, at home after the session). After some practice, the performer might be invited to suggest modifications to the tape and together you can re-tape the script. Always encourage the performer to evaluate the effectiveness of each imagery session.

3   If you have the time, you may wish to repeat this exercise before commencing the coaching session.

1   For more detail of how to use imagery skills, you are referred to the other mental skills packs, available from Coachwise Ltd (0113 231 1310).

Your performer may find it helpful to use the Imagery Evaluation Form provided, so you may wish to photocopy it before use. You may wish to adapt this form for your sport or for use in conjunction with your training log.

Imagery evaluation form

- Date: • Place:
- Focus of imagery (ie action, scene, tactic):

- Was the imagery: internal, external, or did it switch from one to the other?

- How vividly did you see
  your images?   Not at all 1 2 3 4 5 Very vividly

- How clearly did you hear
  any sounds?   Not at all 1 2 3 4 5 Very clearly

- How vividly did you feel
  sensations associated with
  body movement?   Not at all 1 2 3 4 5 Very vividly

- How aware were you of
  your emotions during
  the imagery practice?   Not at all 1 2 3 4 5 Very aware

- How vividly were you
  able to detect smells?   Not at all 1 2 3 4 5 Very vividly

- How easily were you able
  to control your imagery?   Not at all 1 2 3 4 5 Very easily

- How confident are you of
  performing this technique/
  drill successfully?   Not at all 1 2 3 4 5 Very confident

- Record any other comments (eg something that worked particularly well, something you might wish to change):

NB If your performer found it difficult, he/she might try focusing on a simple sports technique (one that is familiar to your performer) in isolation and try to re-experience as many sensations associated with it as possible. The performer should then use imagery to perform this technique mentally in various settings (eg in isolation, in training, in competition). Once competent at this, the original images can be recalled and practised.

This script, and others similarly developed for different aspects of performance, can then be used so imagery can enhance various aspects of performance and preparation.

Phase D: Use of Imagery in Competition

1 Your performer should now identify a particular technique or action about which he/she lacks self-confidence (eg one which he/she finds difficult to use in competition). Ask your performer to summarise what he/she finds difficult performing this technique/action:

```
Technique/action:


Difficulties:

•


•


•

```

2 Has this performer successfully used this technique in the past? If you do not know, ask your performer. If the answer to the last question is yes, go straight to Step 5 (Page 83); if the answer is no, move on to Step 3.

3 Your performer may need to model the imagery practice on another performer who has successfully performed this technique. If this is not possible, video footage of a successful performance may help. You should help your performer identify a suitable model (eg someone with similar levels of skills and physical/mental qualities). It is important that your performer can identify with this model[1]. An example from tennis is given in Table 10 over the page to help you.

---

1   However similar two performers may be, there will always be individual differences.

Key Points to Observe	Examples
Footwork	Move feet directly to the path of the ball Foot movements are fast and positive
Balance and weight transfer	Ensure weight is on the back foot as prepare for shot Transfer weight as ball is hit
Angle of racket face on contact	Racket face is closed and finishes upwards as the ball is hit
Degree of hip and shoulder rotation	Hips and shoulders turn sideways as weight is on back foot Hips and shoulders open as weight is transferred and ball is hit
Speed of movement	Fast swing for effective top spin Strong wrist snap
Position of head	Keep head still during strike and follow-through
Follow-through	Racket head finishes high

Table 10: Example of modelling backhand top spin return of serve in tennis

These are all visual prompts and to be effective, the performer would need to use internal and external imagery. Other sensations could include: the feel of the racket (the person modelling this shot would need to describe this), the sound of ball on strings and on the playing surface, the sound of performer's own footwork, the sound of the opponent's serve.

Once your performer has identified a model performer to provide a suitable image, he/she should use a checklist similar to the one provided in Table 10 to guide this observation.

4 Your performer should now observe the model performance and focus on the key points identified in the checklist (if necessary and time allows, your performer may note these down on the checklist). This may need to be repeated several times. This descriptive list will help your performer use imagery skills to replay this image, focusing on the key points. Once your performer has a clear image of this successful performance, the image of the model performer should be replaced with one of him/herself successfully performing the same skill (and still focusing on the key points). Once this has been achieved (your performer can see and feel him/herself perform the technique), this can be used to prepare for and reinforce physical practice.

5 Your performer should now set a goal for using imagery to review this successful performance, noting all the relevant sensations he/she can recall. These can be recorded using the sheet provided:

Imagery record sheet[1]
Technique:

Visual prompts:

Sounds:

Sensations of touch:

Feelings:

Smells:

Imagery can now be used in a number of ways to help the performer cope with this difficult technique in competition. For each of the suggestions in the preceding panel, the basic method is primarily the same; the emphasis of the imagery varies according to the specific needs of the performer[2].

1   You may wish to photocopy this before using it.

2   For more details of how to use imagery, you are referred to other packs available from Coachwise Ltd on 0113 231 1310.

6　With the performer, you can now identify when and how imagery might be used to improve self-confidence in competition. The summary sheet in Table 11 might help to focus your thinking.

Occasion	How to Use Imagery
Day before competition	Going through tactical options Image successful performance
Warm-up	Focus on start of competition/other key points Reinforce successful performance
During competition (eg during breaks)	Pre-play next part of performance Successfully replay mistake
After competition	Review key aspects of performance and correct errors Review tactics and alter as necessary

Table 11: Summary of use of imagery in competition

Identify how and when and then set a goal to help the performer to use this in competitions. Remember to monitor the effectiveness of the imagery by using some form of report sheet.

Competition imagery checklist

Chosen technique/aspect of performance:

How imagery used (to do what?):

How successful was this use of imagery (and why)?

Changes to this imagery for use in the future:

Recap

Imagery can be used in a number of ways.

Before sessions/competitions, imagery can help to:

- rehearse tactics
- develop contingency plans
- practise difficult aspects of performance
- alter physical readiness levels

After sessions/competitions, imagery can help to:

- assess and correct errors
- evaluate strengths and weaknesses
- reinforce successes
- amend tactics

To help performers develop their imagery skills, you might find the following checklist useful:

Questions to ask yourself

- How easily are your performers able to use imagery?
- Which senses do they prefer?
- Do they use internal or external perspectives (visualisation)?
- How can I modify training to encourage the use of imagery?
- How can I help performers use imagery before, during and after competitions?
- Do my performers set goals for their imagery practice?

Programme Five: Building Self-confidence Using Routines

AIM

To help performers develop routines to improve their self-confidence.

Many top performers report using routines to prepare for performance. Routines are used both in the preparation for competition and specific aspects of the event. Routines can incorporate any aspect of performance – physical, psychological, technical and tactical. Whatever aspect, they should enable the performer to prepare and perform with more consistency and less anxiety. Before embarking on this programme, ensure you have read the section on routines in Chapter Two (Page 38).

By the end of this programme, you should be able to:

- help performers determine when routines will be beneficial
- identify what routines performers currently use
- determine the key components of a routine
- help performers develop and use their own routines to aid self-confidence.

In this programme, you will need to work with your performers on several occasions:

Phase A: One session outside coaching session time (allow one to two hours).

Phase B: Over a number of coaching sessions (number and time-frame dependent on action agreed).

Phase C: Develop competition routine and use in competition.

Phase A: One session outside coaching session time (allow one to two hours)

❏ Many performers and coaches develop routines – consciously or unconsciously – some are useful ways to improve performance, other simply provide some familiarity. It may help to read the example from a player taking a kick at goal in rugby.

Routine for goal kick

- Perfectly place ball on sand/stand
- Measure out four strides behind and to the left of the ball
- Sight ball and posts, assess weight and direction of kick
- See and feel a perfect strike
- Relax arms
- Feel the tempo of the kick – imagery can be especially useful here
- Deep breath – focus on small strike point on the ball
- Lead off with non-striking foot
- Firm placement of non-striking foot at set point in relation to ball
- Clean, sharp strike
- Smooth follow-through
- See and feel a perfect strike
- Feel the tempo of the kick
- Smooth follow-through.

Ask your performer to describe the things he/she typically does or likes to do (routines) on the following occasions:

- Prior to a training or competition event:

What	When	Why	Benefits

- During a training or competition event (may need to specify specific techniques/actions where use is made of routines):

What	When	Why	Benefits

- After a training or competition event:

What	When	Why	Benefits

You probably found your performer has a number of routines that help manage his/her time and focus attention on key tasks. How aware were you of these routines?

Each performer may have his or her own routines for:

- the day before the event
- immediately before the event
- during the event
- during breaks in the action
- after the event.

You will probably find that the timing of some of these routines is generally under the performer's control (eg when he/she eats breakfast before an event, when the warm-up is begun), whereas others will need to be used when the situation demands. Whenever routines are used, they should be performed as consistently as possible.

2 Selecting one routine example (to be most effective, choose one from within the event) and work with your performer through the following guidelines:

> 1 Describe in detail what a successful execution of this technique/action looks and feels like (imagery can help you relive the experience and help identify detail) This should include all phases (eg the preparation, execution and follow-through):
>
> -
> -
> -
> -
> -
>
> 2 Highlight the most important points (no more than three) relating to this technique/action on which you want to focus. Mark these on your list.
>
> 3 Use imagery to replay this technique/action several times, focusing as you do on the successful execution of these key points (you may find it useful to identify a key word for each of the key points[1]). Examples of key words might include:
>
> - perfect
> - tempo
> - smooth.
>
> Your key words:
>
> -
> -
> -
> -
> -

---

1 See **Mental Skills: An Introduction for Sports Coaches** for further information on using key words.

Phase B: Over a number of coaching sessions (number and time-frame dependent on action agreed)

1 Your performer should now have a blueprint of this technique or action to use whenever called upon. The next stage is to use this blueprint as the basis for a specific routine for use first in training and, once competent, in competition.

For each of the key points, your performer should develop a set pattern of actions which result in the successful execution of this part of the technique or action (eg to feel the tempo of the kick, the player numbered his approach steps and strike, saying the numbers to himself and touching his leg with his finger in time with the appropriate tempo).

In your performer's next (or most appropriate) training session, he/she should select one key point and use the accompanying routine at each appropriate opportunity.

> You and your performer should now set a goal for using a specific routine in training:

2 Each time the technique or action is required, he/she should ensure this routine is performed effectively (if necessary, using the key word to trigger the appropriate actions).You can help your performer by providing feedback and advice on the execution of this routine. This performer can then be helped to modify his/her routine if appropriate. Once confident and competent, other aspects with their accompanying routines can be added.

3 The performer should monitor this routine regularly (eg the performer may review the routine at regular intervals, assessing the value of each aspect of the routine to ensure it is still effective). Feedback from the coach can provide useful information to assist this process.

Phase C: Develop and use routine for competition (one to two hours)

Once all the key points have been mastered and the routines honed in training, the same routines can be used in competition. Focusing on what your performer does on the day of competition, work with him/her to complete the following competition checklist:

Competition checklist

1 Before leaving for the event:

- How many hours do you like to have between getting up and the start of the event?
- What do you like to do between getting up and leaving for the event (eg eat a specific meal, use imagery to rehearse the event, relax reading the newspaper)?

2 Travelling to the venue:

- How do you usually travel (eg by car, bus, train)?
- What is the typical length of time spent travelling to the venue?
- What do you do in this time (eg drive, sleep, talk, read)?

3 Arrival at the venue:

- How long before the start of the event do you prefer to arrive?
- What do you like to do on arrival at the venue (eg check competition details, check equipment)?

4 Prior to the event:

- How long before the event do you like to change for competition?
- Do you prefer to be alone or with others at the competition venue?

5 After changing, how much time is there before you warm-up and how do you like to use this time?

6 Add any other aspect of the pre-event routine that has been missed:

NB You might find it useful to identify any aspect of this routine in which the coach plays a significant role (eg coach talks to performer when travelling to the event). Make a note of these on the competition checklist.

2 The competition routine should build in various means of coping with unexpected eventualities (the what ifs). Complete Table 12 by adding your own what ifs (some examples are provided).

What if...	Contingency
There is a change of start time	Have a radio (to prevent boredom or anxiety) and an effective relaxation technique to use
I have equipment problems	Carry spares and a repair kit
I am delayed getting to the venue	Use imagery drills to use as a mental warm-up and a short version of a physical warm-up

Table 12: What ifs

3 You should try to ensure this routine is catered for whenever your performer is competing at home or away (eg staying in a hotel, travelling to a new venue). This may mean checking meal menus, identifying travel options and checking the venue (eg to identify quiet places where your performer can relax before the event). Knowing this has been done enables your performer to focus on his/her preparation and arrive at the event as well prepared as possible.

Your performers will have more confidence in their routines if they monitor their use and reaffirm their effectiveness on a regular basis. Check:

- each element of the routine is still needed (some aspect may have been altered or should be altered)
- the routine is carried out according to the checklist (eg component actions, sequence)
- the routine has not become a prop which would create anxiety if for some reason it could not be used (ie its use was dependent on factors that cannot always be controlled).

This is where your role is vital. You can observe your performers and help monitor their routines against the checklists (it may be beneficial to video some routines to allow performers to reinforce the routine blueprint or amend as appropriate). Note down one goal for helping your performers develop and use routines:

Goal for using routine:

Recap
You might find the following checklist useful when developing routines:

Questions to ask yourself
- What routines do my performers currently use (and could these be developed further)?
- What are the key components of their routines?
- When are the key points in training and competition when routines would be helpful?
- Does the competition day routine allow for any eventuality (ie is there built-in flexibility)?
- Do performers use their routines on every (appropriate) occasion?
- Are the routines monitored (by performer or coach)?

Programme Six: Building Self-confidence through the Use of Mental Skills

AIM

To integrate mental skills for enhancing self-confidence into your performers' training programmes.

In the preceding sections you identified your performer's strengths and weaknesses and helped your performer develop mental skills to enhance self-confidence. However, this is just the beginning. Self-confidence must be nurtured constantly and the mental skills your performer has begun to develop need to be used appropriately throughout training and competition programmes.

By the end of this chapter, you should be able to:

- identify with each performer which mental skills best develop his/her self-confidence

- establish how chosen mental skills will be integrated into training programmes

- plan, conduct and evaluate the mental skills components of a series of coaching sessions.

For this chapter, you will need to work with your performer for one to two hours outside normal coaching sessions.

Having worked through this pack, you will now probably want to make key decisions (with your performers), such as the following:

- Which mental skills are most appropriate to build into training?
- Which performers most need to use these skills?
- When in the training programme should these skills be introduced?
- How long will it take for these skills to benefit performance?

You and your performers should now be in a position to answer these questions.

There is no simple answer and the decisions you make will depend on:

- the demands of your sport (training and competition)
- your performer's mental skills profile
- the time available to you and your performer.

To help you begin making these decisions, work through the following.

1 With your performer, profile his/her ability to use the mental skills in this pack (complete the profile, scoring using the methods described on Pages 56–59)

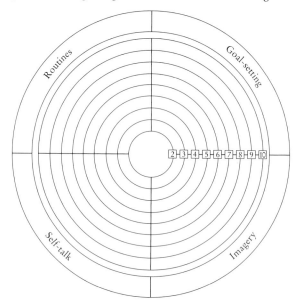

Figure 11: Mental skills profile

2 Ask your performer to what extent he/she feels each mental skill helps build or maintain self-confidence (score this on the profile using a different colour) and to what extent he/she likes to use each skill (now he/she has had a chance to practise each). Mark this on the profile in yet another colour. It might be helpful as part of your continuous monitoring and evaluation of progress, for your performer's mental skills to be profiled again at a suitable point in the programme (eg in three months time or the end of your next phase of training). This will help you and your performer reset priorities for developing these skills.

3 Over the next few months, you and your performer will have particular priorities for training and competition. These will relate to factors such as your performer's current performance level (eg fitness, skill, tactics, mental skills), current stage in the training programme, training goals and competition goals.

Identify your performer's priorities over the next three months for his/her training/competition programme in each of the following aspects of performance (you may want to refer back to the table on Page 57). If any are not priorities, simply leave blank:

Physical fitness:

-
-
-

Technical/skill development:

-
-
-

Tactical development:

-
-
-

Mental skills:

-
-
-

Other areas in need of improvement:

-
-
-

4 Where do each of these priorities fit within the time-frames provided? Where a priority spans over an extended period, identify what will be done towards this priority at each stage – two examples are given in Table 13.

	This Week	This Month	Next Three Months
Fitness objective: Improve reaction time	Specific session to improve reaction time	Improve reaction time.	Improve reaction time. Reaction time test
Specific goal: Test all performers' reaction times.	Develop specific reaction time drill and use in one session.	Adapt and use drill as part of all speed sessions.	Re-test all performers' reaction times, provide feedback to performers.
Mental skills objective: Improve concentration	Concentration exercises to do at home	Develop use of key/triggerwords in training.	Simulated competition/ distraction training.
Specific goal: Use concentration exercise for 15 minutes each day.	Use concentration exercise for 15 minutes each day.	With performer, identify suitable trigger words and use in all training sessions.	Progressively introduce key distractions into simulated competitions (one per week).

Table 13: Examples of objectives and specific goals
for fitness and mental skills work

Now complete the following chart:

	This Week	This Month	Next Three Months
Objective: Goal:			
Objective: Goal:			
Objective: Goal:			
Objective: Goal:			

For each objective, you should agree a SMARTER goal with your performer (remember, goals should be set for all important aspects of performance). Write these goals under the objectives identified in the table.

Remember – the achievement (or non-achievement) of each of these goals (as well as other factors such as competition achievements, feedback from the coach, opponent's achievements) has a potential influence on your performer's self-confidence.

5 For each goal set for training/competition, note the mental skill/s most likely to be helpful in achieving it (an example is provided).

Priority Goals	Mental Skills of Most Assistance to Performer
This week To introduce and practise a new tactic in training	Goal-setting Imagery
Next Month To use new tactic in simulated competition	Self-talk Imagery
Three Months To use this tactic in competition	Self-talk Routines

6 Go back to the mental skills profile for this performer (Figure 11 on Page 96). Check the performer is competent and confident to use the mental skills required in the programme by asking 'Does my performer have a low score in his/her profile on any of the mental skills identified in the right-hand column?'.

If yes, you may need to go back over the relevant section in the pack and spend more time developing this particular skill. If any of these skills has yet to be developed, you should check Activity 3 (Page 10) to remind yourself of when these skills might be introduced. If the answer is no, you will need to ensure these mental skills continue to be fostered and developed in the training/competition programmes. How can this be done?

7 For each goal set for next week, outline the plan for the coaching session(s) you will run to achieve this goal. Include within this plan how mental skills will be used by your performer. An example is given in the following panel.

Session plan

Goal: To improve steeplechase hurdle technique at race pace (athletics).

Process goals: To run eight repetitions at race pace.
                    To alternate right and left leg lead when hurdling.
                    To use positive self-talk at key points throughout the session.

Session plan: Five minutes for mental rehearsal.
                    Twenty minutes for warm-up.
                    8 x 400m (with 200m jog recovery) with four steeplechase
                    barriers each lap at race pace (coach to observe).
                    Emphasise spotting the barrier (correct approach stride
                    pattern), accommodating the barrier at race pace.
                    Fifteen minutes for cool-down.
                    Fifteen minutes for feedback.

Mental skills for self-confidence:
Performer to:
- re-state primary performance and process goals during warm-up
- use imagery and self-talk before the warm-up to mentally rehearse good hurdle technique at race pace
- use warm-up routine which emphasises hamstring, groin, lower back flexibility
- use positive self-talk at set points in the approach to each barrier
- use imagery in cool-down to replay hurdling and correct technique errors.

Coach to:
- evaluate performance and provide positive feedback on technique
- agree with performer goals to progress technique further.

Now produce a similar plan for one of your performer's sessions (use your performer's mental skills profile to determine which mental skills are most appropriate at present):

Session plan
Goal:

Process goals:

Session plan:

Mental skills for self-confidence. Performer to:
•

•

•

Coach to:
•

•

8 You can now repeat this process for each session to develop your performer's action plan for using mental skills. You will need to monitor progress and amend the plan if necessary. As the programme develops, it might be necessary to utilise other mental skills[1].

It is essential that your performer takes responsibility for using mental skills (both within and outside training sessions). You can help identify which mental skills may be most useful but it is the performer who must use them (and to do this effectively, he/she must believe in their worth to performance).

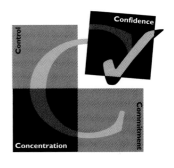

1　For a full listing of other mental skills packs, contact Coachwise Ltd (0113 231 1310).

Final Summary

Using mental skills is not a quick fix to building self-confidence. Their use will only be effective if the skills are regularly practised and time is built into the programme to monitor and adapt their use. As your performer develops, he/she will build up a menu of mental skills. Like all aspects of performance preparation, you and your performer should emphasise different skills as and when required.

Coaches will need to provide the necessary support and guidance to help performers develop, practise and hone their mental skills. The amount of help and support will vary. However, ultimately it is the performer who must take responsibility for the development and use of mental skills and strategies, in the same way they must be encouraged and empowered to take responsibility for every aspect of performance.

The mental skills programmes in this pack are an invaluable aid to self-confidence. However, remember that confidence is inextricably linked with success. The more your performer is able to achieve success, the greater will be his/her self-confidence. Your role is to help this to happen by developing a training climate in which progress can be made and regular success experienced.

Recommended Further Reading

Bull, SJ (1991) **Sport psychology: a self-help guide.** Marlborough, Crowood Press. ISBN 1-85223-568-3.

Butler, R (1996) **Performance profiling.** Leeds, National Coaching Foundation. ISBN 0-947850-36-8.

Hardy,L, Jones, G and Gould, D (1996) **Understanding psychological preparation for sport: theory and practice.** Chichester, Wiley. ISBN 0-471-95787-9.

Loudis, L, Lobitz, C and Singer, K (1988) **Constructive thinking: changing your self-talk.** In Skiing out of your mind. Huddersfield, Springfield Books Ltd. ISBN 0-947655-42-5.

Mace, R (1995) **With netball in mind.** Sports Council. ISBN 0-9524742-0-4.

Morris, T (1997) **Psychological skills training in sport.** Leeds, National Coaching Foundation. ISBN 0-947850-78-3.

Sellars, C (1996) **Mental skills: An introduction for sports coaches.** Leeds, National Coaching Foundation. ISBN 0-947850-34-1.

Weinberg, R (1988) **The mental advantage: developing your psychological skills in tennis.** Champaign, IL, Leisure Press. ISBN 0-88011-293-X.

Contact Coachwise Ltd (0113 231 1310) for an up to date listing of other NCF mental skills packs.